Blockchain for Business 2019

A user-friendly introduction to blockchain technology and its business applications

Peter Lipovyanov

BIRMINGHAM - MUMBAI

Blockchain for Business 2019

Commissioning Editor: Sunith Shetty
Acquisition Editor: Devika Battike
Content Development Editor: Athikho Sapuni Rishana
Technical Editor: Joseph Sunil
Copy Editor: Safis Editing
Project Coordinator: Kirti Pisat
Proofreader: Safis Editing
Indexer: Tejal Daruwale Soni
Graphics: Jisha Chirayil
Production Coordinator: Nilesh Mohite

First published: January 2019

Production reference: 1250119

Published by Packt Publishing Ltd.
Livery Place
35 Livery Street
Birmingham
B3 2PB, UK.

ISBN 978-1-78995-602-3

www.packtpub.com

`mapt.io`

Mapt is an online digital library that gives you full access to over 5,000 books and videos, as well as industry leading tools to help you plan your personal development and advance your career. For more information, please visit our website.

Why subscribe?

- Spend less time learning and more time coding with practical eBooks and Videos from over 4,000 industry professionals

- Improve your learning with Skill Plans built especially for you

- Get a free eBook or video every month

- Mapt is fully searchable

- Copy and paste, print, and bookmark content

Packt.com

Did you know that Packt offers eBook versions of every book published, with PDF and ePub files available? You can upgrade to the eBook version at `www.packt.com` and as a print book customer, you are entitled to a discount on the eBook copy. Get in touch with us at `customercare@packtpub.com` for more details.

At `www.packt.com`, you can also read a collection of free technical articles, sign up for a range of free newsletters, and receive exclusive discounts and offers on Packt books and eBooks.

Contributors

About the author

Peter Lipovyanov is an experienced investment banker and venture investor currently focusing on blockchain projects and crypto-assets. A firm believer in the potential of blockchain technology to change the world for the better by facilitating financial inclusion across the globe and improving the efficiency of financial markets and other sectors of the economy, he has been involved in several promising blockchain projects building decentralized applications. His passion for education also led him to create a bestseller online course about the fundamental principles of blockchain technology and its business applications, which is the basis for this book.

About the reviewers

Samanyu Chopra is a developer, entrepreneur, and blockchain supporter with wide experience of conceptualizing, developing, and producing computer and mobile software. He has been programming since the age of 11. He is proficient in programming languages such as JavaScript, Scala, C#, C++, and Swift. He has a wide range of experience in developing for computers and mobiles. He has been a supporter of Bitcoin and blockchain since its early days and has been part of wide-ranging decentralized projects for a long time. You can connect with him via LinkedIn.

Iqbal Singh is the CEO and founder of Immanent Solutions, a management-consulting and blockchain solutions firm based in Chandigarh, India. He is also the chief blockchain architect for the Blockchain Solutions Asia 2018 conference. Iqbal possesses 15 years' extensive hands-on experience in blockchain, IT, **Internet of Things (IoT)**, AI, automation, and the RIA industry. Iqbal has provided business solutions for Bitcoin, Ethereum, Ripple, and R3's Corda blockchain platform. He heads 30 professional teams working in the fields of data science, algorithms, cryptography (SHA256, X11, and Script), blockchain, **initial coin offerings (ICO)**, Coin, ERC20, Exchange, BTC, and ETH Expert Architect.

Narendranath Reddy is an experienced full-stack software engineer and Hyperledger Fabric expert with a proven track record of helping enterprises to build production-ready blockchain-backed applications. He is an experienced innovator and creative thinker. He has won four hackathons on blockchain and is a keynote speaker. He regularly speaks about blockchain and distributed ledgers and is currently working as a blockchain developer at Block Gemini, Dubai. Previously, he worked as a blockchain developer at Innominds, Hyderabad, and as a software developer at UST Global in Trivandrum and Madrid.

Packt is searching for authors like you

If you're interested in becoming an author for Packt, please visit `authors.packtpub.com` and apply today. We have worked with thousands of developers and tech professionals, just like you, to help them share their insight with the global tech community. You can make a general application, apply for a specific hot topic that we are recruiting an author for, or submit your own idea.

Table of Contents

Preface

Blockchain for Business 2019 is a comprehensive guide that enables you to use various blockchain functionalities to extend your existing business models and make correct and fully-informed decisions. You will learn how decentralized applications are transforming various business sectors, and that they are expected to play a huge role in the future. You will see how large corporations are already implementing blockchain technology. You will then learn about various blockchain services, such as Bitcoin, Ethereum, and Hyperledger, in order to understand their use cases in various business domains. You will develop a solid and fundamental understanding of blockchain architecture.

Moving ahead, you will get to grips with the inner workings of blockchain with detailed explanations of mining, decentralized consensus, cryptography, smart contracts, and many other important concepts. You will delve into a realistic view of the current state of blockchain technology, along with its issues and limitations, as well as their potential solutions, which can take it to the next level.

By the end of this book, you will be well-versed in the latest innovations and developments in the emerging blockchain space.

Who this book is for

This book is for financial professionals, business executives, managers, and enthusiasts who are interested in learning more about blockchain technology in various business domains. This book will help boost your existing business models using blockchain services. No prior experience of blockchain is required.

What this book covers

Chapter 1, *Bitcoin, Blockchain, and Cryptoassets*, introduces the reader to the content of the book. It gets the reader up to speed with the latest blockchain developments, including price action, and covers some exciting blockchain projects and use cases.

Chapter 2, *A Brief History of Money*, covers the definition, main functions, origins, and evolution of the concept of money from barter trade to commodities, gold standard, fiat, and finally digital and cryptocurrencies. It examines these concepts with some basic economic theory and historical examples to enable the reader to logically make sense of the current developments in digital and cryptocurrencies.

Chapter 3, *The Birth of Bitcoin and the Advantages of a Decentralized Payment System,* introduces the circumstances around the launch of Bitcoin and the chain of events and innovations that lead to its creation. It explains the advantages of using a decentralized system instead of a centralized system.

Chapter 4, *Five Forces of Bitcoin – #1 Blockchain*, introduces the five technologies driving Bitcoin, namely blockchain, cryptography, consensus algorithm, peer-to-peer network, and software code base. Then, it goes on to describe the blockchain technology in more detail.

Chapter 5, *Five Forces of Bitcoin – #2 Cryptography*, defines cryptography and describes its historical evolution and some key concepts that are relevant to Bitcoin and cryptoassets in general.

Chapter 6, *Five Forces of Bitcoin – #3 Consensus Algorithm*, discusses the heart of the Bitcoin blockchain, the Proof-of-Work consensus algorithm, which solved the double-spending problem in a decentralized way for the first time in history, and thus enabled the existence of decentralized payment networks.

Chapter 7, *Five Forces of Bitcoin – #4 P2P Network*, discusses Bitcoin's peer-to-peer protocol and network and the different types of nodes in the network, including full nodes, and SPV nodes.

Chapter 8, *Five Forces of Bitcoin – #5 Software Code Base*, discusses Bitcoin's software code base and its scripting language. Different types of wallets, blockchain explorers, and other applications are also presented. The chapter also discusses the programmability of Bitcoin, which enables features and decentralized applications such as digital asset registers, trade finance, and crowdfunding.

Chapter 9, *How Ethereum Took the Idea of Blockchain to the Next Level*, introduces Ethereum and its founder, Vitalik Buterin. The chapter discusses how it was launched, looks at its main features, and examines how it builds upon Bitcoin. Then it goes on to explain Ethereum's Turing-complete smart contracts and the Ethereum Virtual Machine.

Chapter 10, *Ethereum – A Global Platform for Decentralized Applications*, presents Ethereum's use case as a platform for decentralized applications with the help of some examples. Then it goes on to present Ethereum's crowdfunding aspect, again with examples. It also discusses Ethereum's bold vision of **Decentralized Autonomous Organizations** (**DAOs**).

Chapter 11, *Blockchains Focused on Specific Sectors and Use Cases*, presents some public blockchains focused on specific sectors or use cases, as opposed to general-purpose blockchain protocols such as Ethereum. Then it goes on to examine the potential impact of blockchain on the financial, consumer, and technology sectors.

`Chapter 12`, *Corporate Blockchains*, discusses the main private permissioned blockchain projects developed by and for large corporations. It describes the differences between this type of blockchain and the permission-less public blockchains discussed previously.

`Chapter 13`, *The Disruptive Potential of Blockchain Technology*, recaps the current state of affairs in the blockchain space and takes a look at the future potential of the technology.

`Chapter 14`, *Blockchain and AI*, discusses the intersection between blockchain and AI and some potential convergence points and use cases. What are the key advantages of blockchain and AI, and how can they be combined? The main thesis is that the convergence between blockchain and AI lies in the automation of tasks and entire business processes to increase productivity and efficiency in the future's shared economy.

`Chapter 15`, *Current Issues and Potential Solutions to Take Blockchain to the Next Level*, discusses the current challenges for blockchain technology, such as scalability, interoperability, governance, privacy, and regulation. Then it presents the set of solutions being developed to overcome these challenges and take blockchain to the next level and, potentially, mass adoption. Some of the main projects trying to develop next-generation blockchain technology are also presented.

To get the most out of this book

A general idea about blockchain would be useful.

Download the color images

We also provide a PDF file that has color images of the screenshots/diagrams used in this book. You can download it here: `http://www.packtpub.com/sites/default/files/downloads/9781789956023_ColorImages.pdf`.

Conventions used

There are a number of text conventions used throughout this book.

Bold: Indicates a new term, an important word, or words that you see onscreen. For example, words in menus or dialog boxes appear in the text like this. Here is an example: "In economics, this is called a **positive network effect**. The larger the network, the more valuable it is."

Warnings or important notes appear like this.

 Tips and tricks appear like this.

Get in touch

Feedback from our readers is always welcome.

General feedback: If you have questions about any aspect of this book, mention the book title in the subject of your message and email us at customercare@packtpub.com.

Errata: Although we have taken every care to ensure the accuracy of our content, mistakes do happen. If you have found a mistake in this book, we would be grateful if you would report this to us. Please visit www.packt.com/submit-errata, selecting your book, clicking on the Errata Submission Form link, and entering the details.

Piracy: If you come across any illegal copies of our works in any form on the Internet, we would be grateful if you would provide us with the location address or website name. Please contact us at copyright@packt.com with a link to the material.

If you are interested in becoming an author: If there is a topic that you have expertise in and you are interested in either writing or contributing to a book, please visit authors.packtpub.com.

Reviews

Please leave a review. Once you have read and used this book, why not leave a review on the site that you purchased it from? Potential readers can then see and use your unbiased opinion to make purchase decisions, we at Packt can understand what you think about our products, and our authors can see your feedback on their book. Thank you!

For more information about Packt, please visit packt.com.

Bitcoin, Blockchain, and Cryptoassets

In this book, you will learn about the amazing world of blockchain. Blockchain is a technology that pretty much took the world by storm in 2017, and it shows no signs of slowing down. Bitcoin, blockchain, and cryptocurrency are words that almost everybody knows these days. These words have entered peoples' minds through mainstream media, which has finally paid some attention to this exciting new technology.

In this chapter, we will cover the following topics:

- An introduction to blockchain
- The key features of blockchain
- The impact of blockchain in industries
- The impact of blockchain on the internet

An introduction to blockchain

What, exactly, is blockchain? **Blockchain** is a rapidly increasing list of records that are linked to each other via cryptography. In simple terms, a blockchain is a record of a particular transaction that is encrypted, secured, and linked to other transactions.

When blockchain started out, it didn't gain much ground. However, by 2017, it was hard not to pay attention to a market that had increased in value by around 50 times over the course of 12 months, from around 15 billion US dollars in January, 2017, to over 830 billion US dollars on 7 January, 2018.

These are eye-watering numbers, but they only represent the value of publicly traded cryptoassets (meaning the currencies that are in circulation), and not the entire supply! A lot of the supply is still locked away and kept by the founding teams, which helps to make Bitcoin as secure as it is now. You will learn more about this in later chapters of this book.

The rise of blockchain

Just like with the internet stocks in 2000 (and pretty much every single asset that has ever existed), blockchain has gone through the boom and bust cycle of markets driven by greed and fear.

Every market participant has probably heard the following terms thousands of times:

- **FOMO**: Fear of missing out
- **FUD**: Fear, uncertainty, and doubt

These terms correctly describe the psychology of the crowds that drive the roller coaster situation in the markets. This is especially amplified in markets dealing in new technologies, where people speculate on the future of such new technologies and startups, especially when these markets are public and global, which means that anyone, from anywhere in the world, can take part 24/7! That's the main reason for the incredible volatility that we have seen in cryptoassets.

Some fun facts are as follows:

- In December, 2017, Satoshi Nakamoto, the publicly unknown founder of Bitcoin, became one of the 50 richest people in the world, with a net worth estimated at around $20 billion, all based on his or her Bitcoin holdings.
- In January, 2018, the cofounder, executive chairman, and former CEO of Ripple, Chris Larsen, made an even bigger jump, becoming the fifth richest person in the world! His holdings in Ripple's cryptocurrency, XRP, were valued at approximately $60 billion. This catapulted him ahead of people like the founders of Google, Larry Page and Sergey Brin, and the founder of Oracle, Larry Ellison. Only Amazon's Jeff Bezos, Microsoft founder Bill Gates, Berkshire Hathaway's Warren Buffett, and Facebook's Mark Zuckerberg were ahead of him at the time.

Since its peak in January 2018, the market capitalization has gone down to the 100-200 billion USD range. While such a fall may be disappointing for some, we should still be reminded of the 15 billion market cap in January 2017. This is still amazing growth in a very short period of time, which has hardly been observed in other industries throughout history.

Key features of blockchain

The cryptoassets and blockchain market is quite possibly the fastest growing industry that the world has ever seen. This has to do with the speed at which information travels nowadays, which is also unprecedented.

So, why is blockchain such a big deal? What is Bitcoin? What are cryptoassets?

The preceding questions were asked by everyone when blockchain was new to the market. Quite often, they were given complicated answers, involving terms such as distributed database, cryptographic keys, hash functions, game theory, consensus protocols, and so on.

But, if you think about it, people were once baffled by terms such as domain name, website, bandwidth, and download. The main point is that blockchain technology is set to reshape the future, and will soon be a part of everyday life, just like the internet is.

Ease of access

Just like the internet, anyone can get involved in blockchain! We've seen people with diverse backgrounds, from all corners of society, getting involved with blockchain and cryptoassets. From the Wall Street tycoon to the average person, and even people with questionable reputations, everyone can enjoy the benefits of blockchain. On top of that, everyone involved has something to say about the glories or the evils of the technology. Even high-profile individuals and world leaders are trying to steer public opinion, in one way or another.

One of the positive effects of all of the media noise that started with the skyrocketing prices and brought blockchain to the mainstream domain, was that it attracted a lot of talent to this space. Thousands of developers and business people have joined the industry and focused their efforts on building blockchain projects. All of this new energy must lead to substantial results and value creation, which will justify some of the hype and market valuations that we have seen. But such fundamental developments and value creation don't happen overnight. They take a lot of time and effort.

Blockchain – the internet of money

The key features of blockchain—security, transparency, decentralization, immutability, and programmability, are combined in a platform, which doesn't need any central authority in order to process transactions, value, and information transfers. By doing so, in a direct, peer-to-peer way, blockchain creates a completely new paradigm for global business.

No wonder there are so many heated opinions and discussions about it; and, oh boy, can it get overwhelming! What this shows is how important this technology is, and what it can bring to the world.

While we call it the **internet of money**, we should remember that blockchain is a layer on top of the internet that is highly effective and efficient for storing and transferring values in a decentralized way.

The hype of industrial companies around blockchain

During the boom of 2017, we saw all sorts of projects and companies claiming to use blockchain for pretty much everything; this just shows an attempt to ride the hype wave. There were even cases such as the New York-based soft drinks company Long Island Iced Tea, which rebranded itself to Long Blockchain Corp, only to see its shares rise by nearly 500%. Such actions definitely don't help anyone, as the company was promptly investigated by the **Securities and Exchange Commission** (**SEC**).

Some of the other developments in the blockchain community were the multiple forks in the largest cryptoasset, Bitcoin, which we saw recently. Forks are basically splits in the network, resulting from differences in the software protocol being run by its participants.

We have seen various actors trying to drive their own versions of Bitcoin forward, and this has resulted in the creation of Bitcoin Cash, Bitcoin Gold, Bitcoin Diamond, Bitcoin Private, and Bitcoin **Satoshi's Vision** (**SV**), among others. Such developments may partly result from a desire to improve the protocol, but they also result from greedy attempts to achieve more control and extract more value from the internet of money. Effective governance of decentralized systems in the presence of multiple (and sometimes, contradictory) interests that have to be balanced is one of the most difficult problems that need to be solved going forward.

Going back to the key benefits of distributed ledgers, removing middlemen and quick and efficient transaction settlement are definitely right at the top. This can enable lots of interesting use cases, from payments and money transfers to property registers and capital markets. Such infrastructures can be public or private, the main differences being in the level of trust embedded in the system. A public network that is open to everyone, where parties don't know each other, needs a different level of security and a different consensus mechanism than a private, permissioned network, where parties are vetted before they are allowed to join. This will be discussed in detail later on.

Impacts of blockchain

Blockchain has the potential to fix many problems on a global scale, and to impact many industries.

There is a large number of industries that have become stagnant, centralized, and inefficient, thereby proving unable to grow economically in their current state, create value, or solve existing problems. In the case of such industries, what we need is a technological revolution, and blockchain is ready to lead the charge!

Impacts in the financial sector

The financial sector will be among the first to be disrupted by blockchain technology. The previous major technological innovations in the financial sector, the ATM and the credit card, were introduced way back in the 1950s and 60s.

Not only that, but according to the World Bank, their most recent study found 2 billion people who are unbanked. That's over a quarter of the entire global population! As you can imagine, this stunts global economic progress significantly. Not to mention that the unbanked people, who are mostly from developing countries, are at a clear disadvantage. It is difficult enough to increase productivity and trade within their own country, let alone transacting with the rest of the world. Many people consider the fees for sending money overseas for these populations unfair. Money transfer services, such as Western Union and MoneyGram, were charging 10% on average in 2008, and 7.5% in 2016. Blockchain technology can disrupt the status quo and bring this to a halt.

It can bring new, efficient solutions—not just for money transfers, but also for global trade finance, clearing and settlement, insurance and securities trading, and many more financial services and products.

But, it's not just the client facing side of finance that blockchain technology can improve. It can also streamline compliance and regulatory functions, such as **anti-money laundering (AML)** and **know your customer (KYC)**.

Impacts in our daily lives

Blockchain technology can also be applied to accounting and auditing, healthcare, the media, consumer goods, logistics and supply chain management, power and utilities, the internet, and even the government. We will delve into these areas in `Chapter 10`, *Blockchains Focused on Specific Sectors and Use Cases*. For now, let's give you a little taste of the ingenious ways that some companies are trying to apply blockchain, in order to change peoples' lives for the better.

The Chinese formula scandal

Do you remember the awful Chinese infant formula scandal in 2008?

300,000 babies fell victim to melamine being added to baby formula. Melamine is a chemical used to produce plastics, which you'll find in your everyday whiteboard. When added to milk, the chemical appears to contain higher protein content, which was a dirty trick that led to many infants being hospitalized.

The effects of this scandal were felt worldwide, and they destroyed the reputation of China's food export industry! At least 11 countries refused to import dairy products from China. Chinese retailers would travel to Australia and other countries to buy huge stocks of their baby formula. And the Chinese government even executed several individuals involved in the scandal. Sadly, this is not an isolated incident. Many other companies use illegal and immoral ingredients in their foods and other consumer products, often being discovered after it's too late.

That's where blockchain technology can come into action. It can help to remedy and prevent counterfeit consumer goods. A startup called WaBi is working on resolving these kinds of problems. By combining blockchain and **radio-frequency identification (RFID)** technologies, they can track and verify the authenticity of all ingredients and components used in consumer goods.

Blood diamonds

Another example comes from a company called Everledger, which is working to resolve the long-standing issue with blood diamonds. Their aim is to track the origin of each diamond and record it on an immutable blockchain database.

Similarly, other startups are aiming to solve the problems of counterfeit art and other luxury goods with blockchain technology.

Gradually, distributed ledgers will become a part of our everyday lives in many different areas, helping to improve the way that we make payments and investments, the way that we register our properties, how we verify our identity, and even the way that we vote in elections.

Impacts of blockchain on the internet

Blockchain can also reform the internet, by bringing in web 3.0 and more.

A less centralized internet with more peer-to-peer interaction will discourage large internet monopolies and circumvent gatekeepers. Decentralization can empower consumers and producers alike, by giving them more control over their personal data and a level playing field in online business. It can also increase the role of **prosumers,** people that both consume and produce goods and services in a system. Some examples include decentralized social networks, and marketplaces, where participants are rewarded for contributing content or sharing and consuming resources at the same time. This is a next-level sharing economy, enabled by distributed applications.

Fully-programmable blockchain networks enable such distributed applications and peer-to-peer marketplaces. We have recently seen many startups trying to build more efficient markets for scarce resources, such as electricity, computer processing power, file storage, and advertising. Whether blockchain technology can be applied successfully to add value to such projects is a matter of scalability, user interfaces, and user experience.

Interoperability with other systems (and the internet as a whole) is also very important, and there are projects trying to build such protocol infrastructures in an efficient way. More importantly, the protocols are the sets of standardized rules adopted worldwide for using in computer systems to communicate with each other. Protocols, such as HTTP and FTP, have formed the base layer of the internet. Such protocols are now being developed for distributed computing systems, such as blockchain. The interaction of these new technologies and the concept of a shared economy is expected to deliver the vision of web 3.0.

Summary

This chapter introduced the basic facts and the latest developments around blockchain technology. You learned about the great opportunities and benefits that can arise from adopting and applying this technology around the world. You also saw some cases of misuse and inappropriate practices, trying to take advantage of the market hype, which will need to be remedied by market participants and regulators.

In the rest of this book, we will go deeper into each of these topics. The book will show you, in detail, how the technology works, as well as its pros and cons. We will delve further into blockchain applications, potential challenges, the solutions to those challenges, and how the technology is expected to evolve in the future. So, let's step into the world of blockchain together!

A Brief History of Money 2

Now that you've had a sneak peek into the enormous body of knowledge that blockchain technology manifests, it is a good time to take a step back and go back to the basics. In this chapter, we'll look at the history of money. If you can grasp how the financial sector reached its current state, then you will better understand why blockchain technology is the natural next step in monetary evolution.

The following topics will be covered in this chapter:

- An introduction to money
- Money – an abstraction of value
- An introduction to fiat currencies
- What happens when fiat currency systems fail
- How blockchain comes into the picture

An introduction to money

A brief discussion of money will help to solidify your understanding of the mix of finance and technology that we have in the world today.

Basically, we should ask ourselves this question: what is money? Let's think about it for a second; we will find that it's not as easy to define as it might seem.

The textbook definition would claim that money has three main functions, as follows:

- A medium of exchange
- A unit of account
- A store of value

If you are still lost with these definitions, we'll be going into more detail about what they mean in the coming sections.

Money as a medium of exchange

Let's look at a simple example of a barter exchange. Suppose that you traded one of your ranch's horses for a cow. What a good deal, right? Now, a week later, you go out for dinner, you finish the meal, the waitress comes over to give you the bill, and you prepare to pay her with a part of the cow that you got earlier! We can imagine that such a situation will not end well!

This is where we need money! Money is your medium of exchange. Often, you cannot trade a good or service for another good or service directly. Money is an intermediate commodity that is universally accepted and has a standard value for all parties. That's why it facilitates value exchanges more efficiently than barter trade.

Money as a unit of account

So, is that all we need money for? Actually, there's more to it. We also use money as a unit of account, meaning that we use it to compare the values of goods or services to those of other goods or services, and to record those values.

For example, when we check out and compare vehicles, we always try to find the most value for our money. We compare these vehicles by using their values, and we decide which one is better suited for us.

Money as a store of value

Money also needs to be a store of value, meaning that it maintains its value, or purchasing power, over time. This eliminates any commodities or objects prone to spoilage or corrosion. For example, precious metals, such as gold, silver, and platinum, are a great store of value, as their shelf lives are essentially perpetual, whereas things such as milk, wheat, or iron, are not such good stores of value.

Another desirable characteristic of money is **scarcity**, which, as the name suggests, means that it needs to have a limited supply. As they say, money doesn't grow on trees. If it did, it wouldn't be money.

To give you a few more examples, consider the following:

- Stones wouldn't make for a very good form of money, because they are around everywhere in nature

- For a community of people who live on a tropical island, shells would not be a good form of money, because it would be so easy to find them on the beach
- Gold, on the other hand, is a rare metal, is hard to find in nature, and is universally appreciated for its aesthetic qualities and its industrial use cases

Gold is also durable. A gold coin will not shatter if you drop it, nor will it bend if you sit on it. However, with the right skills and tools, it is divisible, it can be turned into things, and it can be shared, if necessary.

Fungibility is another key feature of money, meaning that all units of the same denomination are interchangeable. Think about a hundred dollar bill, which is perfectly replaceable by another hundred dollar bill.

Finally, money needs to be easy to move and carry around, in order to facilitate trade; here is the only advantage of paper money over gold coins and bars. This is even more true in the case of electronic money, since everyone has access to the internet!

Money – an abstraction of value

Now, let's consider the concept of money as an abstraction of value.

Money is as old as human civilization, and civilization itself is reliant on possessing ways through which they can exchange, account for, and transfer value. What once started as barter trade (trading goods for goods) was replaced with using standardized token money.

Gold and silver were the first universally accepted natural choices for money. Actually, they fit the bill so well that they were the primary form of money across the globe for centuries, and have been instilled in human culture. When we say gold, the first thing that comes to mind is value or wealth.

After this came paper money, a more user-friendly way to carry and move around value, as compared to precious metals. China was the first to adopt it, in the seventh century. However, the western world didn't catch up on this monetary innovation until Marco Polo introduced it to Europe in the thirteenth century. Even then, the first European banknotes weren't issued until the seventeenth century. It took people several centuries to accept the new paradigm at the time, and to shift from gold and silver coins to banknotes backed by the same precious metals as the widely used form of money.

The gold standard

This led to the birth of the gold standard. Back then, the banknotes themselves didn't hold any intrinsic value, such as gold and silver coins do. Instead, paper money was backed by precious metals (such as gold and silver), stored in a treasury vault somewhere, such as Fort Knox. The banknotes represented the right to collect those precious metals from a bank. This was more convenient than taking a wheelbarrow of gold bullion to the post office to pay the mortgage!

This was the case until 1944. At the end of World War II, yet another related system was introduced under the Bretton Woods agreement, which was the gold exchange standard. This meant that many countries fixed their national currencies' exchange rates to the US dollar, which was, in turn, convertible to gold, at a fixed rate. This system can be better illustrated by the following diagram:

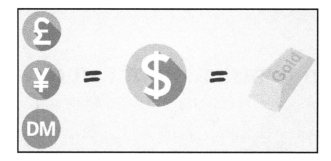

Not only that, but this convertibility was no longer available to individuals or companies, but only to central banks. However, the Bretton Woods system ended in 1971, when the US dollar convertibility to gold was terminated. Since then, paper money has no longer been backed by gold (or anything else tangible), but just faith!

An introduction to fiat currencies

Welcome to the world of fiat currencies! How does paper hold any value if it's not backed by anything? Well, that's where concepts such as legal tender come in.

The fiat system, which we still use today, has governments assign value to a currency, declaring it a **legal tender.** This means that a government decides whether a medium of payment will be recognized for financial transactions, trade settlement, or commerce in a country or jurisdiction.

The legal tender concept is just another manifestation of the perception of value characteristic of money. The key difference here is that with commodity money, there is a tangible resource to which the money supply can be pegged. And with fiat money, the money (or the quantity of money in circulation) is a much more discretionary subject to central banks' policies. Therefore, the margin for human error (involuntary or voluntary mismanagement) is larger.

Proponents of the fiat system argue that it enables more monetary policy tools to stimulate or control the economic cycle, by varying the money supply and interest rates. These tools have been used with varying degrees of success in the past.

Some fiat currencies, such as the US dollar and the Euro, are recognized internationally, and are used for global trade, because they are backed by some of the most credible governments and largest economies in the world.

Other fiat currencies have suffered from hyperinflation and lost value, after people lost faith in them. A well-known example is the **Zimbabwean dollar** (**ZWD**), with its 100 trillion denomination banknote, which we will learn about in the following section. However, large and leading economies, such as Germany (Weimar Republic, in 1922-1923) and China (1943-1945), have gone through periods of hyperinflation, due to excessive fiat money printing without the backing of sufficient, real economic resources.

What happens when fiat currency systems fail

A fiat currency has value because a government uses its power to enforce that value, or because exchanging parties agree to its value. It's not hard to see how problems could occur in this scenario. Let's look at some examples of when the fiat currency system backfired under the control of irresponsible or corrupt governments, prone to economic and political mismanagement.

At the time of the independence of Zimbabwe from British colonial rule in 1980, the ZWD was worth about 1.25 US dollars. Soon after, inflation started to creep up, and it got completely out of control when President Robert Mugabe began confiscating land from the white farming community in 1998, resulting in a nearly total collapse in food production and the decline of foreign investment.

In order to help pay for the government's expenditures, the Reserve Bank of Zimbabwe started to print more and more banknotes, with higher and higher face values. As a result, the annual inflation rate rose from 32% in 1998 to 231,000,000% in July 2008, when official statistics stopped being reported. After that, it was estimated by international economists that the hyperinflation peaked at a staggering annual rate of 89.7 sextillion percent (89,700,000,000,000,000,000,000%), in mid-November 2008. The peak monthly rate was 79.6 billion percent, which is equivalent to a 98% daily rate; in other words, prices were pretty much doubling every day:

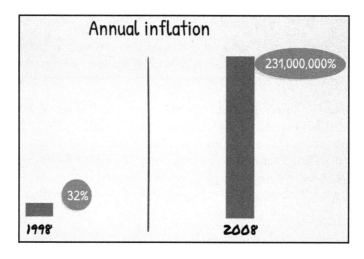

In February 2009, the ZWD was redenominated for the third time in the last three years, at a ratio of 1 trillion old ZWDs to 1 new ZWD. This happened only three weeks after the $100 trillion banknote was issued.

In April 2009, the ZWD was completely abandoned in favor of only using foreign currencies.

Once one of the richest countries in Africa, Zimbabwe descended into economic chaos, largely due to its government's policies. This is an extreme example of how the trust in a fiat currency can be lost, leading to economic turmoil. In Zimbabwe, the collective illusion quickly turned into a collective disbelief.

This is not an isolated example of a currency crisis, though. There are many countries around the world where local currencies hold hardly any value, and people prefer to keep their savings in the so-called hard foreign currencies, or other alternatives, such as gold, and, most recently, Bitcoin!

Currently, Venezuela is undergoing a period of raging inflation of its own. In January 2018, inflation was 84% for the month, implying an annualized rate of 150,000%, meaning that prices would double every 35 days. This is an estimated figure, as the local government has stopped reporting official data. Some estimates for the current rate of annual inflation go even higher, to around 450,000%!

Now, the Venezuelan government has come up with an innovative proposed solution for a stable currency—the Petro, a government issued cryptocurrency, running on blockchain and backed by the country's oil reserves. The Petro is intended to be a legal tender in Venezuela, which is becoming the first country in the world to issue a sovereign cryptocurrency. It remains to be seen how successful this experiment will be. Such a centrally issued cryptocurrency is a far cry from the decentralized nature of Bitcoin and its digital siblings. However, it should also be noted that, with its actions, Venezuela is recognizing and reaffirming the great advantages and potential that blockchain holds.

How blockchain comes into the picture

Now, it's time to ask ourselves this question—Is blockchain the next logical step in monetary evolution?

"There are 3 eras of currency—commodity based, politically based, and now, math based."

- Chris Dixon

The preceding quote shows how the concept of money has evolved over the years.

Throughout all of these stages, we have had an idea of value in our mind, but it has evolved hand in hand with our civilization and technology, from something that you can touch and actually use; to something that you can touch, but cannot use (except for trade); to just an abstract idea. As you can see, the form has changed, but the idea of value has always remained the same, and we represent and communicate the idea of value in terms of money.

This abstraction of value brings us to the next evolutionary step: digital cryptocurrencies, powered by blockchain technology. Similar to the fiat system, this form of money has value because people believe in it. But there is more to it than just a government promise. Promises made by people have been broken many times throughout history. Here, we have solid science, mathematics, and computer hardware, guaranteeing that blockchain works as expected. The following diagram better illustrates the evolution of money over the years:

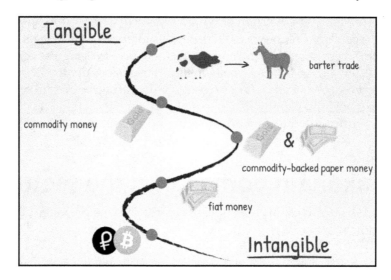

In this new system, we have a mathematical algorithm controlling the money supply and putting strict limits and costs on it, similar to a gold standard. Is this system perfect? No; as we saw recently with the countless Bitcoin forks, having an open source software controlling the money supply, in a large and complex decentralized ecosystem, has given rise to some complicated governance issues. If every disagreement leads to the creation of a new version of the currency, this could lead to a lot of confusion.

So, even though they were initially called cryptocurrencies, Bitcoin and its digital siblings are not really currencies, as they stand now. Rather, they are digital commodities or assets; that's why cryptoassets is a more appropriate term for them. A currency needs to be stable, in order to perform its functions well. We still live in a fiat world, where all transactions are denominated in fiat currency. Even though there are ways to pay with Bitcoin and more, they are still converted into fiat at the point of sale. And their exchange rate is subject to huge volatility on a daily basis. That's why many electronic payment companies have started to issue stable coins: digital currencies pegged to a fiat currency, but using blockchain as the underlying payment processing infrastructure, as opposed to the legacy one. We'll cover such solutions in more detail in later chapters, after you are more familiar with how blockchain works.

Summary

In this chapter, you saw how the idea of money has evolved throughout history, from a more tangible to a more intangible concept, with each stage having its pros and cons. From barter trade, we moved to commodity money, through to commodity-backed paper money, and on to the fiat money that we use now. This was a historical journey, from real goods and commodities to numbers on a computer screen, representing value and money!

In the following chapter, we'll look at how the technologies underpinning Bitcoin emerged, and how they were put to work together. This mix of technology enables value, information transfers, and record-keeping in a decentralized way, without the need for any central agents or middlemen.

3
The Birth of Bitcoin and the Advantages of a Decentralized Payment System

In the previous two chapters, you discovered what money is nowadays, an abstraction of value. We also noted that the concept of money has become less and less tangible over the years, up to the creation of digital money.

In this chapter, we will look at what stands behind blockchain technology, and how it allows us to create and work with digital money.

The following topics will be covered in this chapter:

- How Bitcoin came into existence
- Projects leading up to Bitcoin
- An introduction to Bitcoin
- How traditional payment systems work

How Bitcoin came into existence

Our core goal is to understand how blockchain functions, and why Bitcoin has become so popular. However, in order to do that, we need to provide a quick recap of some macroeconomic events that took place in recent history. Bitcoin's launch during the global economic and financial crisis was one of the most important things to ever happen in the history of money.

Blockchain technology is commonly referred to as the **internet of money** or **value**. Let's begin by providing an overview of the chain of events that led to the emergence of Bitcoin, which was the first globally recognized application of blockchain technology.

The Bitcoin whitepaper was published in October 2008, the year when the global economic and financial crisis hit the world. Coincidence or not, Bitcoin seems perfectly designed to address many of the deficiencies of fiat money.

A little-known fact is that the genesis block of the Bitcoin blockchain, where its first transaction was recorded, contains a hidden message by its creator, Satoshi Nakamoto. The text quotes a headline from the British newspaper *The Times*, which shows a proof of the date when the Bitcoin blockchain was launched, and it states the following—*The Times, 03/Jan/2009, Chancellor on brink of second bailout for banks*.

Aside from proving the date of the genesis block, this message seems cleverly designed to express the tragic state of the global financial system at the time. It also implies the importance of the proposed solution as a stepping stone towards an improved monetary system. Being embedded in the genesis block, and given the immutable and robust nature of the Bitcoin blockchain, that message stands as an everlasting reminder for future generations.

The beginning of the economic crisis

Since the dissolution of the Bretton Woods agreement in 1971 and the introduction of the modern fiat currency system, the world entered a new era of mostly freely fluctuating foreign exchange rates. National central banks started to implement various monetary policies to manage money supply in their respective economies. Monetary policy objectives may have had various nuances around the world, but a common, widely accepted theme has been inflation targeting. This is done in order to provide healthy, stable, low inflation rates, facilitating sustained economic growth. By targeting low inflation rates, central banks around the world aim to create stable economic conditions, providing the right incentives for consumers' and businesses' economic activity, in the absence of huge price swings up or down.

This strategy has had varying degrees of success throughout the years and across different countries.

In the same period, there has been unprecedented credit growth and accumulations of debt globally, which led to the sub-prime mortgage crisis, credit crunches around the world, and the global economic recession. When banks started to fail and investments in new economic ventures decreased, governments and central banks around the world realized that they needed to do something to stimulate the economy; hence, the rounds of **quantitative easing (QE)** started.

This resulted in an unprecedented supply of new fiat money entering the economy, and close to zero (and, in some cases, even negative) interest rates, which is another economic phenomenon unheard of in standard economic theory and practice.

The idea behind printing so much money was to stimulate the economy and save the financial system from collapse. However, as happens frequently, there were also some side effects of such policies. The prices of real and financial assets, such as global equities and real estate, rose significantly, thereby debasing the store of value aspect of fiat currency.

The birth of Bitcoin

Social inequality has also increased meaningfully since the global recession. Again, this is due to the huge amount of liquidity, or new money supply, entering the global financial system and pouring into asset classes, such as real estate, stock markets, and venture capital. This, of course, inflated their prices. As these asset classes are normally mostly accessible to wealthy investors that use the services of savvy asset managers, the net effect was a growing wealth gap. On the other hand, the majority of people with little or no investable assets, whose income is mostly based on labor wages, haven't nearly experienced the same wealth effect. This has probably had implications on the global political landscape in recent years, but since political economics is not our scope here, we won't cover it.

Long story short, in the midst of such unprecedented and critical events in the global economic and financial landscape, Bitcoin was born.

Projects leading up to Bitcoin

In parallel with the economic events that we just described, the technology community has been undergoing an evolution of its own. Many brilliant technical minds have been working hard on solving problems to enable secure digital currency payments.

In fact, the Bitcoin whitepaper references prominent scientific publications, such as *An Introduction to Probability Theory and its Applications* by William Feller, published by John Wiley and Sons, Inc., in 1957; the *BMoney* paper by Wei Dai, published in 1998; and the *Hashcash - A Denial of Service Counter-Measure* paper, written by Adam Back in 2002.

Before we dive into the Bitcoin blockchain, we should tell you that the concept of digital currencies is not entirely new, and certainly was not invented with Bitcoin. Satoshi, the founder of Bitcoin, built his project considering and utilizing existing scientific research, carried out in several disciplines. He also added a few innovative solutions of his own, and put everything to work together in a brilliant way.

The following is a summary of some of the notable scientific breakthroughs preceding Bitcoin, and some of which Bitcoin builds upon:

- In the early 1980s, David Chaum, a brilliant mathematician, published several research papers on cryptography and its applications in electronic payment systems. Then, a few years later, he founded DigiCash Inc., developing the eCash software, which enabled users to store money in a digital format, cryptographically signed by a bank. Users could also spend such digital money at any shop accepting eCash. There was no need to open an account with the vendors or to give them your credit card numbers. This can be better illustrated with the following diagram:

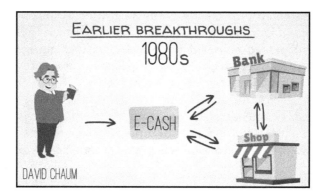

- In 1998, Wei Dai, a computer engineer, published a paper proposing what he called B-Money, an anonymous, distributed electronic cash system based on a peer-to-peer network, where nodes (the computers participating in the network) collectively maintain and update a ledger of transactions. The importance of Wei Dai's work is highlighted by the fact that Satoshi Nakamoto referenced B-Money in his original Bitcoin whitepaper. This can be seen in the following diagram:

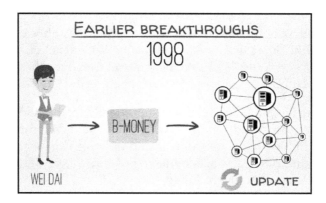

- In 1997, Adam Back introduced his Hashcash concept. This was designed as a system to prevent email spam. The idea is that, in order to send an email, users' computers need to do some calculations first. As it takes time, energy, and processing power to do such calculations, this adds a cost base to sending an email. Such a cost is not expected to be prohibitive for legitimate email users, as the number of emails they send is reasonably low, while it should discourage spammers, who send thousands of emails daily. For this purpose, hash functions are used, which are a special type of mathematical function. A computer would need to calculate a hash function multiple times, in order to find the required solution to a computational puzzle.
- A concept similar to Hashcash was introduced even earlier, in a 1992 paper by Cynthia Dwork and Moni Naor, titled *Pricing via Processing or Combatting Junk Mail*. Their main idea was to require a user to compute a moderately hard function, in order to gain access to a shared resource, thus preventing frivolous use.
- A closely related subject, the term **Proof-of-Work** was first introduced in 1999, by the computer scientists Markus Jakobsson and Ari Juels. They define it as a proof that a certain amount of computational work has been done in a specified period of time.

A similar idea was implemented in Bitcoin's Proof-of-Work algorithm, as described in Satoshi's white paper:

> *"The network timestamps transactions by hashing them into an ongoing chain of hash-based Proof-of-Work, forming a record that cannot be changed without redoing the Proof-of-Work."*

So, basically, Proof-of-Work is a proof that a certain amount of computational work has been done by a computer. Such work has an identifiable cost to it. Therefore, Proof-of-Work is a proof that external resources have been invested in doing a certain amount of work, and thus, the work done arguably has value.

- Around the same time, Nick Szabo, another prominent computer scientist, came up with the concept of BitGold, which was never implemented in practice, but has been called a direct precursor to the Bitcoin architecture. Nick Szabo described his idea as follows:

> *"I started thinking about the analogy between difficult-to-solve problems and the difficulty of mining gold. If a puzzle took time and energy to solve, then it could be considered to have value. The solution could then be given to someone as a digital coin."*

In a BitGold network, solved cryptographic puzzles would be sent to the community, and, if accepted, the work would be credited to the person who had done it. This would then translate into newly generated digital coins. A new puzzle would only be released once a solution to the previous one was found and accepted by the community. In the process of solving such tasks, community members who come up with solutions would own growing amounts of new digital property. This aspect of the system provided a way for the network to verify and timestamp new coins. Unless a majority of the parties agreed to accept new solutions, they couldn't start on the next puzzle. Nick Szabo made a good point about digital value creation, given that the computational work required in the process is unforgeable. Until a network participant came up with a solution, no extra coins were issued. Therefore, this digital money supply was scarce, difficult to produce, and could be securely stored and transferred. This is a very close concept to Bitcoin mining.

- Another prominent figure in the early cryptocurrency community was Hal Finney. He was a computer scientist, who later participated in the first ever Bitcoin transaction with Satoshi. Hal Finney made a valuable contribution to the growing body of research into digital currency systems, introducing **Reusable Proof-of-Work**, building upon the Proof-of-Work concept introduced earlier. The purpose of Reusable Proof-of-Work was as token money. Just as a gold coin's value is underpinned by the value of the raw gold needed to make it, the value of a Reusable Proof-of-Work token is guaranteed by the value of the work done in order to generate it. And, as we already know, the value of the work is backed by the real-world computer resources and electricity required to do it. He referenced Nick Szabo's Bit Gold idea of digital goods that are provably costly to create.

All of the scientific milestones that were mentioned previously, and several others, contributed a great deal to the advance of digital currencies and the birth of Bitcoin. Most of the previous projects had one or more features of Bitcoin, but none of them had a complete and effective solution to the problem that Bitcoin eventually solved. They mostly relied on a centralized payment settlement system, not much different from the way the traditional financial system works.

Now, with all of this background in mind, let's dive straight into the workings of Bitcoin.

An introduction to Bitcoin

So, what is Bitcoin? Perhaps it's best to start with the words of its creator, Satoshi Nakamoto, which we find in the original whitepaper, *Bitcoin: A Peer-to-Peer Electronic Cash System*. It states the following:

> *"A purely peer-to-peer version of electronic cash would allow online payments to be sent directly from one party to another without going through a financial institution. Digital signatures provide part of the solution, but the main benefits are lost if a trusted third party is still required to prevent double-spending. We propose a solution to the double-spending problem using a peer-to-peer network. The network timestamps transactions by hashing them into an ongoing chain of hash-based Proof-of-Work, forming a record that cannot be changed without redoing the Proof-of-Work."*

To understand what Satoshi meant with these words, we'll have to explain a few important concepts in more detail.

First of all, Bitcoin's creator placed a great emphasis on the network's peer-to-peer nature. This means that Bitcoin is a decentralized network. There isn't any central party responsible for managing the system. It is a truly democratic platform, open to everyone to participate and contribute. The network of Bitcoin can be seen in the following diagram:

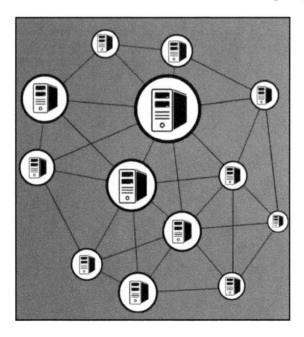

As Satoshi Nakamoto suggests, the main idea is to have a system without intermediaries that prevents double-spending with the sole involvement of peers on the network.

Until Bitcoin came around, people could not transact directly with each other over the internet without the involvement of a trusted central party. This is because money transmitted electronically isn't the same as other types of information or digital items. You can take a picture and share it with all of your friends on Facebook, but if you have one dollar and want to share it, you cannot send the same one dollar to each one of your friends.

Double-spending can occur when a user tries to spend the same unit of digital currency twice at the same time, effectively multiplying the money that one has by copying it. This is equivalent to counterfeiting currency in the real world.

If double-spending were to exist, the system would not be an effective store of value, and would lack one of the fundamental prerequisites of money, which is scarcity.

Imagine that you are shopping online, and you want to pay using digital currency. Let's suppose that you have a few coins in your wallet. You like a brand new movie on Amazon, and an audiobook on Audible. You want to have both, but the digital money that you have is sufficient for only one of the two items. What if you were able to use the same digital currency to buy both goods?

Before the Amazon or Audible guys know that you have spent the same coins twice, you will be able to click **Purchase** on both websites within a few seconds, and download the products.

Double-spending and how Bitcoin resolved it

Double-spending is a problem that is unique to digital currencies, because digital information can be reproduced relatively easily. Physical currencies do not have this issue, as they cannot easily be replicated. You probably have an idea of all of the protections in place that secure the banknotes in your wallet from anyone simply copying them.

Bitcoin was the first digital currency system to solve the double-spending problem in a decentralized way, and the solution is indeed elegant and ingenious. All transactions on the Bitcoin network are recorded on a shared public transaction log, also known as a blockchain database. On the Bitcoin blockchain, the network timestamps the first transaction where the owner spends a specific coin, and rejects any subsequent attempts by the same owner to spend the same coin, thus eliminating double-spending. The network is smart, and its blocks keep records of who owns a coin right now, and who has already spent it.

At this point, you may think: OK, but this doesn't seem like such an incredible innovation. After all, they just keep a record of all transactions, in order of appearance, in a ledger, just as any bank or similar financial intermediary does.

Well, yes, but the uniqueness of this solution is that the transaction verification and recording is done in a decentralized way, by the entire network, rather than by a single, trusted central authority.

Satoshi's goal is to eliminate the third parties that can become potential central points of failure. Hence, any such verification must be performed by the peers themselves, and not by any middlemen.

In the next section, we'll discuss in more detail how the Bitcoin's decentralized model is different from the existing legacy financial infrastructure.

How traditional payment systems work

As anticipated, our goal here is to discuss how the participants in a blockchain network ensure that the double entry accounting principle is taken care of. We'll also show how this solution is different from the other existing solutions of the legacy financial system.

In the Bitcoin blockchain, payments are settled through a so-called consensus mechanism, which works based on economic incentives rooted in game theory. Confused? We will explain it in simpler terms in the following paragraph.

The consensus process aligns the interests of all network participants, so that their best course of action is to support the truthful verification and record-keeping of all transactions. We'll cover the consensus mechanisms in more detail later on. For now, here's what Satoshi himself wanted to share about this issue:

> *"The problem of course is the payee can't verify that one of the owners did not double-spend the coin. A common solution is to introduce a trusted central authority, or mint, that checks every transaction for double spending. After each transaction, the coin must be returned to the mint to issue a new coin, and only coins issued directly from the mint are trusted not to be double-spent. The problem with this solution is that the fate of the entire money system depends on the company running the mint, with every transaction having to go through them, just like a bank.*
>
> *We need a way for the payee to know that the previous owners did not sign any earlier transactions. For our purposes, the earliest transaction is the one that counts, so we don't care about later attempts to double-spend. The only way to confirm the absence of a transaction is to be aware of all transactions. In the mint based model, the mint was aware of all transactions and decided which arrived first. To accomplish this without a trusted party, transactions must be publicly announced, and we need a system for participants to agree on a single history of the order in which they were received. The payee needs proof that at the time of each transaction, the majority of nodes agreed it was the first received."*

So, the root of the problem is to secure a consensus process through which all participants in the network are on the same page at any given time. This process must be so robust that all participants trust it with their money. The simple solution is to introduce a trusted central authority to run the ledger of transactions, just like a bank. History has shown many times that such central parties, or middlemen, can present a risk of their own, and have been compromised far too often.

Therefore, Satoshi goes for the more difficult solution: to secure and maintain decentralized consensus in a global payment system. In fact, this problem is so complex that nobody had ever solved it before.

Let's run through a few examples of how different existing payment systems work.

Electronic transfers in banks

Banks have been the traditional payment intermediaries for centuries. They maintain accounts for their customers, process payments, and provide other financial services. They also manage the relevant financial infrastructure. Currently, electronic bank transfers are done in the following way:

1. An account holder orders a bank transfer from his or her bank account to another bank account.
2. The sending bank uses IBAN and BIC codes to direct the payment to its destination. **IBAN** stands for **International Bank Account Number**. It is an international system for identifying bank accounts to facilitate cross-border transactions. **BIC** stands for **Business Identifier Code**, which is also used for payment identification.
3. The sending bank transmits a message to the receiving bank via a secure communication network, called **SWIFT**. This stands for **Society for Worldwide Interbank Financial Telecommunication**. The message contains instructions to the receiving bank, to make the payment to the destination account.
4. The banks involved must hold reciprocal accounts with each other, or the payment must be routed through a corresponding bank, which is another intermediary holding accounts with both banks on the opposite sides of the transaction.
5. The actual transfer is not instantaneous; funds may take several hours, or even days, to move from the sender's account to the receiver's account.
6. All of the banks participating in the transfer get fees for the services provided, from the sender and the recipient.

This whole process can be summarized with the following diagram:

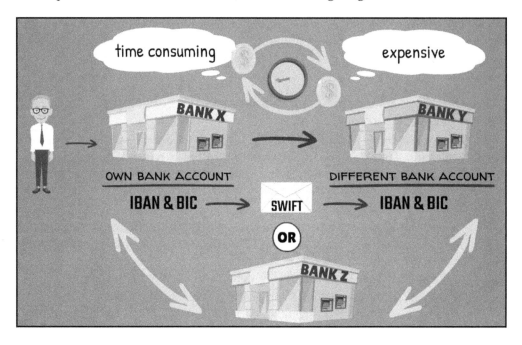

Credit and debit card transactions

Credit and debit card transactions involve an even longer list of intermediaries. In addition to the payer's and payee's banks (where they hold accounts), there are a bunch of other payment processors on both sides, and the Visa or Mastercard network in the middle. Visa and Mastercard hold huge market power in this value chain, and this is easy to see in their profit margins. Everyone can check that out in their financial accounts, as they are publicly listed companies.

A basic credit or debit card transaction involves the following steps:

1. A consumer initiates a payment at the **point of sale** (**POS**) to a merchant or retailer. This is done via a POS terminal (if in a store) or via a website (if online).
2. The merchant then transmits the sales data to a merchant acquirer. The merchant acquirer can be the bank where the merchant holds an account, or another payment processor. Many banks participating in card schemes outsource this part, which is basically a back-office function, to external providers.

3. The merchant acquirer routes the transaction request data through a card network, such as Visa or Mastercard.
4. The card network sends the transaction request data to the card issuing bank.
5. The card issuing bank remits the funds back through the card payment network.
6. The card payment network passes on the funds to the merchant acquirer.
7. Finally, the merchant acquirer credits the merchant's deposit bank account.
8. Needless to say, all of the intermediaries involved in the process get paid substantial fees for passing the money on through the system.

This system can be summarized with the following diagram:

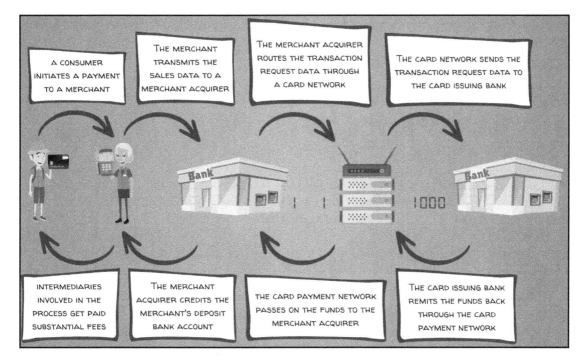

This process can involve more steps if banks on both sides decide to outsource more of the back-office transaction processing to third-party intermediaries. The whole cycle can, in theory, be completed in 12 hours, but it typically takes 3 to 4 days, depending on the individual contractual agreements between the various intermediaries involved.

Transactions in PayPal

PayPal functions as another electronic payment intermediary. It is an internet company with global presence. Its services are mainly targeted at e-commerce, connecting customers and merchants. All parties using PayPal and holding accounts with it can send payments to each other through the system. PayPal also integrates with the legacy banking and credit card payment infrastructure.

PayPal is not regulated as a bank, because it doesn't operate a fractional reserve system similar to what banks operate. This is related to the activity of taking deposits, making loans funded by these deposits, and keeping only a fraction of the deposits in reserve. This obviously creates credit risks for deposit holders. Since PayPal doesn't do that, it follows lighter regulations as a money transmitter. This model is quite centralized, is similar to the banking model, and is subject to all of the risks associated with it.

Differences between centralized and decentralized payment systems

To summarize, designing a centralized payment architecture is much easier than designing a decentralized one. However, the centralized model presents security threats from hacks, because there is a clear and attractive target for such attacks. A centralized system also presents a more expensive and inefficient solution for customers, because it tends to create monopolies, or cartels. This concentrates market power in the hands of a small group of intermediaries, which can extract disproportionately large values, in the form of transaction fees. The customer outcomes resulting from the legacy financial infrastructure are expensive, slow transactions. This sector has not seen any major innovations in a very long time, and it is ripe for disruption.

In contrast, a decentralized payment network, such as Bitcoin, implements the more difficult solution of decentralized consensus in transaction processing. This design enables it to deliver a much more efficient solution for all parties involved. Payments go directly from peer to peer, and security and processing are guaranteed by the entire network. Funds are sent and received in a matter of minutes. All of the network participants maintain a consensus of the current state of the transaction ledger, at all times.

Summary

Sounds great, doesn't it? As you saw in this chapter, direct, peer-to-peer interaction is always a superior solution, for all parties involved. There are no rent-seeking intermediaries stuck in the middle to extract value from the counterparties. Now, we have the technology to do that in payments, as well as in any other type of transaction involving value transfer or record keeping!

You learned about how Bitcoin came into existence, and what it does. We also compared it to traditional banking systems.

Now, if this solution seems interesting to you, let's go ahead and develop a deeper understanding of how Bitcoin works!

4

Five Forces of Bitcoin - #1 Blockchain

In the previous chapters, we learned about the history of money, the rise of Bitcoin, and the hows and whys surrounding Bitcoin. In this chapter, we will begin our journey of an in-depth review of Bitcoin. This chapter will cover the following topics:

- Introduction to Bitcoin's five forces
- The first force – blockchain
- Different types of blockchain

Introduction to Bitcoin's five forces

Now that we know what double-spending is, and how Bitcoin resolves this issue, we are ready to continue further and provide a holistic view of Bitcoin's architecture and ecosystem.

The main pillars of Bitcoin are the following fundamental technologies and concepts:

- Blockchain or **distributed ledger technology (DLT)**
- Cryptography
- Consensus mechanism rooted in game theory, which, in this case, is Proof-of-Work
- Peer-to-peer network
- Software code base

We call this framework Bitcoin's five forces.

This framework can be seen in the following diagram:

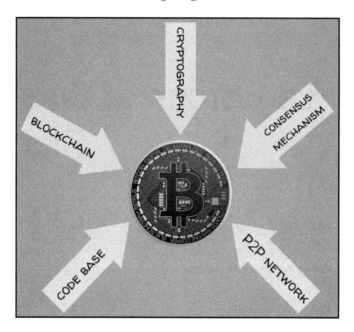

In the next five chapters, we will delve into the specifics of each of these areas and will explain how they are combined to make Bitcoin's mechanism tick. Stay tuned, as things are getting really interesting!

The first force – blockchain

Finally, we got to the point where we can give a straight answer to the question, which everyone has been asking and which is central to this book—what is blockchain?

Blockchain is a decentralized database, which is distributed over a computer network, with each computer in that network storing an identical copy of the same database filesystem. In the context of financial transactions, this is also referred to as DLT because a ledger is an accounting book or a collection of financial records.

In finance, we use a ledger to record all accounting related to a specific entity. A company's bank account would have a ledger that contains many, many transactions. Every time money comes in, or goes out, a new entry would have to be registered in the ledger. In the same way, a blockchain distributed ledger keeps the same information related to a series of transactions across multiple computers, forming a peer-to-peer network.

Why blockchain is better

The idea of hundreds or thousands of computers storing the same file does sound a bit strange at first, doesn't it? It wouldn't be a surprise if your first thought was redundancy. But such redundancy provides security and ensures there is no central point of failure in the entire system. It protects from attempts to manipulate the system by bad actors.

This in turn provides the opportunity to eliminate any centralization or, in other words, to cut out the middlemen. Such decentralized blockchains work through a consensus mechanism or algorithm. There are different types of consensus algorithms and we'll cover the main ones later on in the book.

For the moment, it's important to understand that these consensus algorithms enable the different nodes (which are basically the participants in the network) to verify new transactions and maintain a uniform view of the up-to-date state of the ledger.

How blockchain works

After new transactions are verified, they are ordered and grouped into blocks, which are then linked to previous blocks. Each new block is built on top of the last block in chronological order.

Each of these blocks is a type of data structure containing information and, more precisely, transaction records. Generally, distributed databases can contain any kind of data, not just financial or economic data, but blockchain's security and design make it especially suitable to use for value exchanges. Hence, the expression that blockchain is the internet of value or the internet of money.

Transactions once put on the blockchain are normally irreversible and their record is permanent and immutable.

New blocks are created at regular intervals of time and are timestamped. Each new block is linked to the chain of previous blocks, hence the term **blockchain**.

We should note that Satoshi never mentioned blockchain in the original whitepaper. He mostly referred to the technology as a Proof-of-Work chain. The closest he came to saying blockchain was with phrases such as the next block in the chain or chain of blocks. The term blockchain was popularized by early Bitcoin companies, such as `blockchain.info`.

Next, we'll dig a bit deeper and discuss why blockchain has the potential to revolutionize the financial and industrial world and how it can improve the communication and informational asymmetries between trading partners.

Different types of blockchain

The usefulness of blockchain technology comes from its security, immutability, and transparency. All the nodes have access to the updated and verified information stored in the database simultaneously, and at all times. These features enable huge potential financial and industrial applications. Both the private and public sectors can benefit from blockchain technology. The following sections focus extensively on such applications and on the way blockchain can transform industries and businesses around the world.

Before we move on, we should mention that blockchain can be classified broadly into two main categories:

- Public or permission-less blockchains
- Private or permissioned blockchains

This can be seen in the following diagram:

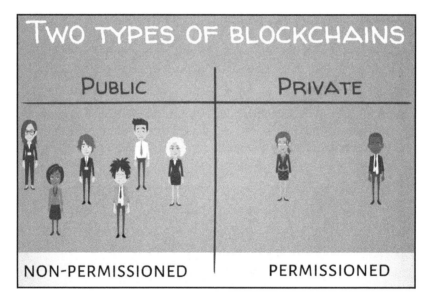

This distinction comes down to who owns the network infrastructure. It is similar to the distinction between the internet and corporate intranets.

Public blockchains

The first type is a public network, which everyone with the right hardware and software can join, support, and use. This is the case with the Bitcoin blockchain, as well as most other public cryptoassets. Here, the benefits of decentralization are the most prominent:

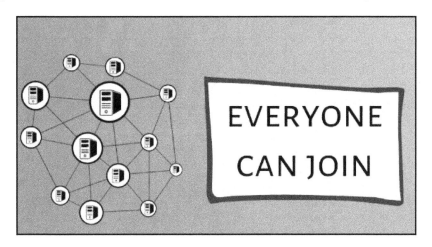

Private blockchains

The second type is owned by an organization or a consortium and is open only to its members or whoever has a permission to access it, which is granted by a gatekeeper. This is much closer to a centralized database, despite the fact that it's still a distributed computer system.

Many large financial institutions and other corporations are actively developing such private blockchains to streamline their operations and benefit from the efficiency blockchain architecture brings about, while still maintaining the privacy required for their internal operations.

Value of blockchain

We've already seen that recording information and organizing it in a ledger resembles an accounting system. Blockchain is a pretty sophisticated accounting system from a technological point of view, but still an accounting system.

A blockchain distributed ledger is stored and maintained by an entire computer network, rather than on a single computer, server, or piece of paper. This is a true element of innovation. If you are still not convinced by the value proposition blockchain brings, consider the fact that the accounting system as we know it today has existed since the 15th century.

Yes, that's right! The double-entry accounting system was introduced by Luca Pacioli in 15th century Italy. It is based on the idea that we have two effects on each side of a transaction: a debit and a credit. This formed the basis for company balance sheets, which are ledgers of assets and liabilities (in other words, what a company owns and what it owes). By codifying these rules, Pacioli provided much needed order and tools to enable enterprises to scale efficiently and track and communicate all of their financial information. This is illustrated in the following diagram:

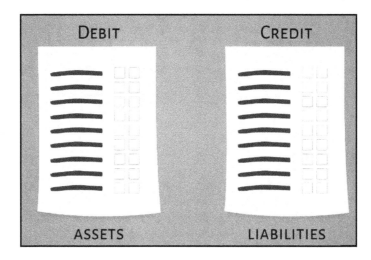

Over time, the complexity of economic transactions has increased, and business enterprises and government bodies can find it handy to have some new tools. In Pacioli's time, business audits were done regularly, on a daily basis. This is not the case anymore. It's impractical to have real-time reporting at the scale at which corporations operate nowadays, at least not in the traditional way. Such lack of accountability has resulted in a number of high-profile corporate disasters and bankruptcies. We've all heard the cases of Enron, WorldCom, and Bernie Madoff's Ponzi scheme, to name a few.

Blockchain can change all this! With its transparency, security, and immutability, it can provide almost real-time audited reporting to stakeholders and regulatory bodies. Imagine how much efficiency and further progress such technology can bring to the world!

Areas where blockchain can be handy

Think about the current state of the banking system. At present all banks are required to do careful due diligence on each and every one of their clients to prevent financial crime, such as money laundering and terrorist financing. This requirement is called **know your customer** (**KYC**) and takes a huge amount of time and paper processing by large teams at each bank. Each bank does KYC separately, so the process can be repeated many times over for the same clients if they have dealings with different financial institutions. Imagine how this process can be optimized if a group of banks shares a private blockchain, where each client is onboarded only once, and all parties can trust the information in it. The regulators and other government authorities could also access and audit this information at any time.

Another straightforward example that comes to mind is securities trading and settlement. Currently, this process involves multiple steps and intermediaries, which makes it expensive and time-consuming. When a buyer and a seller want to trade a security, such as a stock, they need the involvement of a stock exchange, clearing house, and often broker-dealers to execute such a transaction. All the trading information also must be recorded strictly and made available for regulatory audit. All the steps involved take at least two to three days until a trade is settled, meaning that the buyer has received the stock, the seller has received the money, and everything is recorded properly. All these processes can be streamlined on the blockchain, thus enabling simultaneous trade execution, clearing, and settlement in a matter of minutes. And again, regulators could check the transaction records instantly at any time.

These are just a couple of examples demonstrating some use cases of blockchain technology that can streamline the financial sector. Various implementations of blockchain technology can fit different purposes, objectives, and industries.

Summary

In this chapter, we learned about blockchain, how it works, why it is important, and where it can be used to improve our daily lives. In the next chapter, we'll get acquainted with another of Bitcoin's five forces—cryptography.

Five Forces of Bitcoin - #2 Cryptography

5

In this chapter, we will learn all about the art of cryptography and how it has evolved with time. We will get to learn how cryptography affects various aspects of the internet. We will cover the following topics in this chapter:

- Introduction to cryptography
- Types of cryptography
- Hash functions
- Digital signatures

Introduction to cryptography

In this section, we will learn what cryptography is and how it has evolved historically.

Now, we get to the crypto part of cryptocurrencies, which is a well-publicized term you've probably heard plenty of times over the last year or so. This sounds a bit mysterious, or, a bit… cryptic… doesn't it? Many of you have probably heard the word **cryptography**, but how many actually know what it involves?

In brief, cryptography is the science of secure communication. It is useful in order to secure private information from being accessed by unauthorized third parties who can potentially act in bad faith. The process involves two main steps:

1. The first step is **encryption**, which consists of scrambling the information, so that only the intended recipient can access it
2. The next step is **decryption**, which is unscrambling the encrypted information in order to access and use it

The encryption and decryption process usually involves mathematical techniques of varying complexity. The value added by cryptography has been recognized a long time ago, and such techniques have been used for millennia.

Uses of cryptography in early times

Julius Caesar is known to have used encrypted messages to communicate with his generals. His technique was simple by today's standards; he used letters that were three positions away in the alphabet after the intended letter. For example, the letters ABC would be represented by DEF. In fact, this encryption method is widely known as the **Caeser cypher**.

Another famous example of the use of cryptography, which has high historical significance, was the Enigma machine invented by the German engineer Arthur Scherbius at the end of World War I. It was commercialized in the early 1920s and the German army adopted it soon after, in order to secure its military communications. The Enigma machine has nearly 159 Quintilian different combinations of characters and numbers (more precisely 158,962,555,217,826,360,000). The Enigma cypher was considered unbreakable at the time and gave an edge to the German army during World War II. However, a team led by the brilliant English mathematician and early computer science pioneer, Alan Turing, managed to crack the Enigma code, which helped the Allies win the war. These events were recreated in the 2014 film, *The Imitation Game*. We'll come across further references to the genius of Alan Turing and his impact on modern computer science in `Chapter 9`, *How Ethereum Took the Idea of Blockchain to the Next Level*, where we discuss the next generation of blockchain technology—Blockchain 2.0.

Next, we'll continue learning about cryptography and we'll provide some important definitions.

Types of cryptography

Now, we'll introduce some important concepts that will help you understand cryptography's role in the world of blockchain.

Cryptographic cyphers are encrypted and decrypted with keys. These keys are basically secret pieces of information or parameters, which typically look like strings of characters. Think about something such as a password or passphrase that locks and unlocks access to an encrypted message. These are actually keys to the cryptographic algorithms and help convert ordinary information (called **plain text**) into unintelligible text (called **ciphertext**) and vice versa. This is shown in the following diagram:

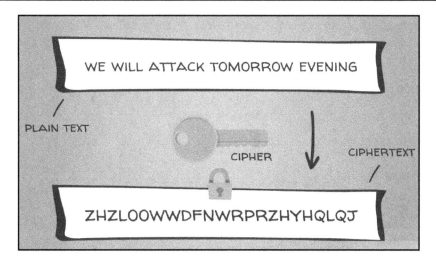

There are two main types of cryptography:

- **Symmetric** (also known as **secret key cryptography**): This is a type of cryptography where the same key is used for both encryption and decryption. This can be seen in the following diagram:

- **Asymmetric** (also known as **public key cryptography**): This is a type of cryptography where the key used for encryption is different from the key used for decryption. This can be seen in the following diagram:

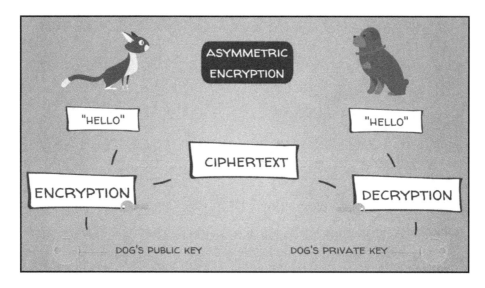

The second type of cryptography, with pairs of public and private keys, is used to provide security and privacy in Bitcoin and other cryptocurrencies. Actually, the Bitcoin blockchain is the largest civilian deployment of public key encryption technology in the world. Only the US Department of Defense makes a larger use of such technology, which says a lot about its merits.

Cryptographic techniques used in Bitcoin

Several cryptographic techniques are used to secure the Bitcoin blockchain, including:

- Public and private keys
- Hash functions
- Digital signatures

Any person who has ever used a cryptocurrency to make a transaction should be familiar with how keys work. Each user has a pair of keys (a public and a private one), which enable transactions on the network. You can see some examples of public and private key pairs in Bitcoin in the following screenshot:

The **public key** is used by the sender to encrypt information regarding the transaction, which then can be decrypted only by the receiver with his or her corresponding **private key**. The public address, which acts like an account, can only receive funds, and is derived from the public key and can be shared openly. The private key must be stored securely and never disclosed as it, and only it, gives access to the user's funds on the blockchain.

If the private key is lost, access to the funds is lost permanently. There is no such thing as a password reset function on the blockchain. Users need to take responsibility for storing and backing up their private keys properly, because there is no central authority on the network that can reverse misplaced transactions or restore private keys. You need to be sure that you understand the implications of any loss of private keys and take all the possible measures to avoid it. You should treat the private keys for your Bitcoin or another cryptoasset with the same care you treat any physical cash, gold, or diamonds you may have. The difference here is that you can back up your private key, as it is a string of characters that can be copied. Therefore, you can print it on paper, save it on a USB memory stick, or use special devices called hardware wallets, such as Ledger or Trezor, that can securely store your private key.

Next, we'll explore another major application of cryptography in Bitcoin—cryptographic hash functions.

Hash functions

In the previous sections, we said that all nodes store identical copies of the blockchain database, didn't we?

And that's an issue that undoubtedly results in a lot of data storage and redundancy. However, it is the price we have to pay in order to obtain a truly decentralized peer-to-peer system without any middlemen.

Moreover, datasets can be different in size, some blocks may have 200 transactions, other blocks may have 500 transactions, and others may have 1,000 transactions. All these transactions also typically vary in the size of the information they contain in terms of kilobytes. The only capacity limit in the Bitcoin blockchain protocol is on the size of each block, which has been 1 megabyte since 2010. It was recently amended to effectively 1.4 MB with the latest upgrade of the Bitcoin software. But again, block sizes can vary up to that limit. You can check for yourselves what blocks look like at blockchain.info or other online block explorers. In the following screenshot, you can see some example blocks:

<< Previous **Blocks mined on: 07/03/2018** Next >>				
Height	Time	Relayed By	Hash	Size (kB)
512383 (Main Chain)	2018-03-07 06:17:58	Unknown	0000000000000000004fb251409e435e981622133a03f117570459a2297af8fa	1,355.22
512382 (Main Chain)	2018-03-07 06:15:58	SlushPool	0000000000000000002c1a88262590390f5d64c9a7805c2118b39dda6de86162	1,061.8
512381 (Main Chain)	2018-03-07 06:14:11	ViaBTC	0000000000000000021b41176525cfa3beba3b8164b5d95e24375cf9ebc67e	1,043.31
512380 (Main Chain)	2018-03-07 06:07:41	SlushPool	0000000000000000002ef5b8413240ec8235a55f32a70d4475fd9660d1882dc1	1,065.79
512379 (Main Chain)	2018-03-07 05:55:34	ViaBTC	0000000000000000053eb904a221441f474e7a0afb438fe35b69f8773f306486	1,037.88
512378 (Main Chain)	2018-03-07 05:49:26	BitFury	0000000000000000004c0785d2dea6b48c6dc7bf12018cdb6af5d8a28c930b	327.41
512377 (Main Chain)	2018-03-07 05:48:23	Unknown	0000000000000000026ee6138c477672c5d2920224036b6839b1a87f16f331571	1,089.99
512376 (Main Chain)	2018-03-07 05:33:14	Unknown	0000000000000000000538baeae8ab6c17e432e5df8a624551c98decbd3af9db8	1,050.8
512375 (Main Chain)	2018-03-07 05:24:20	BitClub Network	0000000000000000028b1db6ac463b46d795b232bdc07901a9c8c4a5703042a	1,045.14
512374 (Main Chain)	2018-03-07 05:19:39	Unknown	0000000000000000001f30b0ea51c59eeb25f1c7c261fb407a7261bc11afef93	1,055.58
512373 (Main Chain)	2018-03-07 05:13:32	Unknown	0000000000000000004f15eb558a0af505839f67a112a6b9569947238Dd666a97	1,178
512372 (Main Chain)	2018-03-07 05:00:17	BTCC Pool	0000000000000000003a015f674a26cb2a96aed65cd1fc9b998551548e298808	1,238.02
512371 (Main Chain)	2018-03-07 04:35:13	GBMiners	0000000000000000046226c3c4d5cc5b6772b1afd55621eb9cb83c7e44fb6cb	1,030.82
512370 (Main Chain)	2018-03-07 04:28:17	ViaBTC	0000000000000000004c1a2b0a1a725d59ed918466271f6c890bd2d9b563e789	1,014.13
512369 (Main Chain)	2018-03-07 04:26:12	Unknown	0000000000000000003bab7fad5944c934797cfcb1608ff417a6a6f739e4f683	1,073.35
512368 (Main Chain)	2018-03-07 04:13:39	AntPool	0000000000000000008920d6630f12665ea357c1b276ed36aff31ffd43e1243	0.28

Hence, a blockchain can benefit from some standardization and rationalization of the data it stores.

A mechanism that allows us to address that are cryptographic hash functions, which are an efficient way to secure data integrity and reduce file size. Hash functions are used to convert input data of any length into a compressed unique fixed length string of characters (also known as a bit string). This output data serves as a unique reference code or digital fingerprint to verify the authenticity of some underlying dataset without the need to actually check the entire dataset.

In practice, this hash function is a mathematical algorithm that maps data of arbitrary size to a bit string of a fixed size (also known as a hash). It is designed to be a one-way function, meaning a function which cannot be inverted and recalculated backward to get to the input data. This can be seen in the following diagram:

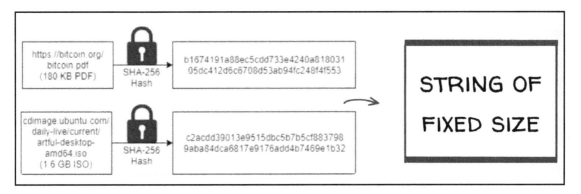

The only way to recreate the input data, if one has the output only, is to attempt a brute-force search of all possible inputs to see if they produce a match. A brute-force search is basically systematically trying all possible combinations to find the solution.

Hash functions are heavily used in the Proof-of-Work blockchain consensus algorithm, as we'll see shortly.

Digital signatures

Another important cryptographic technique used in Bitcoin are digital signatures. They are used for authentication of the origin of transactions on the blockchain. They enable the receiver to verify that the transaction received was originally sent by the sender using his or her private key. This process again includes mathematical calculations. Surprise, surprise!

Basically, the digital signature is generated out of the sender's private key being processed through a digital signature algorithm. The resulting code output is then attached to the signed message and acts like a signature. It designates the sender of the message. Each transaction will have a different digital signature, which is generated through the digital signature algorithm to increase security. It is impossible to generate a valid signature for a party without knowing that party's private key.

Please note that, we use the words transaction and message interchangeably, because transactions on the blockchain are basically messages broadcasted through the network. When you send cryptocurrency to another person, you are basically sending them a message.

Furthermore, digitally signed transaction messages are unforgeable, meaning they cannot be intercepted and modified or reproduced while in transit.

Digital signatures are also non-reusable and they cannot be separated from a transaction message and used for a different message given that the algorithm creates a new signature for each transaction.

To conclude the topic, let's put these cryptographic solutions into the words of the great Satoshi himself:

> *"We define an electronic coin as a chain of digital signatures. Each owner transfers the coin to the next by digitally signing a hash of the previous transaction and the public key of the next owner and adding these to the end of the coin. A payee can verify the signatures to verify the chain of ownership."*

Summary

Alright! We covered some important topics involving a great deal of multi-disciplinary science. The good news is that most of this science has been built into the Bitcoin architecture in an elegant and effective way by Satoshi, so that the system runs smoothly. The only thing you need to take care of, personally as users, is to protect your private keys. Please, do make sure you fully understand the importance of this for your own financial health!

Now, we are ready to move on to the next brilliant engineering solution that powers Bitcoin—the Proof-of-Work consensus algorithm.

6
Five Forces of Bitcoin - #3 Consensus Algorithm

In this chapter, we will find out what makes the Bitcoin blockchain machine tick in a decentralized way. We are going to take a deep dive into the consensus mechanism of Bitcoin called Proof-of-Work and see what it has to do with complex math problems and mining. We will cover the following topics in this chapter:

- The Byzantine Generals' Problem
- The Proof-of-Work consensus algorithm
- Decentralized consensus and game theory

The Byzantine Generals' Problem

The Byzantine Generals' Problem is actually an abstract way to describe a problem in computer systems introduced in a 1982 paper of the same name. The problem states that reliable computer systems must be able to function effectively in the presence of faulty components that may send conflicting information to different parts of the system. This issue is even more acute in decentralized computer networks.

This is illustrated in the following diagram:

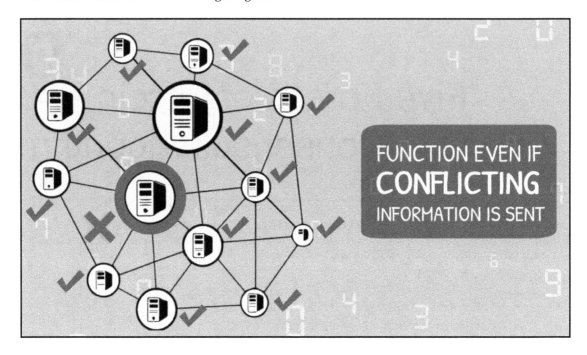

Let's imagine the following thought experiment.

The Byzantine army has surrounded an enemy city. The army is organized in several units. Each unit is commanded by a general. All these generals need to come up with a coordinated plan of action, but they are located away from each other and can communicate only via messages. To make things more complicated, one or more of the generals may be traitors. Such potential traitor generals can send misleading messages and try to disrupt any coordinated plan of action, be it attack or retreat. To find a successful solution to this conundrum, the Byzantine army needs to find its path to coordinated action, one way or another. This experiment can be seen in the following diagram:

To achieve this, the Byzantine army needs some algorithm that works effectively toward a coordinated outcome when the majority of loyal generals follow it, while some traitors don't.

The Proof-of-Work consensus algorithm

Now that you know the problem, let's see the solution, which is called the Byzantine fault tolerance algorithm. This algorithm involves game theory and math.

The first and foremost practical implementation of the Byzantine fault tolerance algorithm came with the Bitcoin's Proof-of-Work. In this case, the generals are nodes on the Bitcoin network, also known as **miners**. A network node is a connection point that can receive, create, store, and send data across a network. In other words, nodes are the connected dots that make up a network.

The important concept to grasp here is that these mining nodes start from the assumption that nobody else on the network can be trusted.

The Proof-of-Work algorithm guarantees network consensus even in the presence of Byzantine non-compliant nodes. Let's see how this mechanism works in Bitcoin.

As we all know by now, Bitcoin is a peer-to-peer network where all activities are done by its users through appropriate software and hardware. These activities include making transactions, receiving transactions, verifying, and transmitting transactions.

Introduction to mining

Now, we will introduce the concept of mining, which many of you have probably heard of. Mining basically involves doing Proof-of-Work and results in generating new coins as a reward for the miner who successfully did this Proof-of-Work first for each new block. Proof-of-Work involves a hefty amount of calculations done by a computer aimed at solving cryptographic hash puzzles. Let's dig into the nuts and bolts of this mechanism to figure out how it works.

First, let's see how miners create new blocks. The following diagram illustrates the creation process:

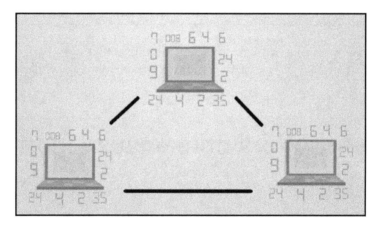

Now, mining nodes collect and aggregate new transaction data. Upon receiving such data, each node independently verifies each and every transaction against a long list of criteria, including the following:

- Tracking the source of the digital money being spent
- Checking for double spending of the same money
- Checking whether the total transaction volume is within the allowed range of 0 to 21 million Bitcoins (as 21 million is the maximum total supply of Bitcoin allowed by the system)

And the list goes on; the Bitcoin software installed on the node performs a number of other checks and balances.

Verified transactions are aggregated into transaction pools, also called memory pools or mempools, where they wait until they are included in a block. Miners check their mempools for any transactions that have been already included in previous blocks. After collecting and arranging verified transactions in a candidate block, the miner needs to construct the block header. This header includes the following main components:

- A summary of all the transaction data in the candidate block
- A link to the previous block in the chain, also known as a parent block
- A timestamp showing the time of creation of the block
- A valid Proof-of-Work

The summaries of block transaction data are done through hash functions, which process data in such a way that results in a standardized unique identification code or digital fingerprint. In this way, the system has a unique identifier for each block of transactions.

The different aspects of a Bitcoin transaction

Here is an example of a block header, as viewed on `blockexplorer.com`:

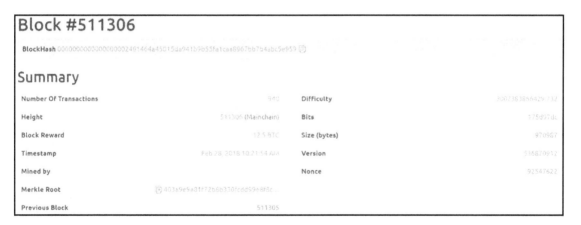

As seen in the preceding screenshot, there is a long alphanumeric string just below the block number called the **BlockHash,** or just **Hash**. Alphanumeric means that it consists of both letters and numbers. This is a type of encoding data and is the output result of processing the block header data present there, through Bitcoin's cryptographic hash function. You may have heard the name of this function, SHA 256, where **SHA** stands for **Secure Hash Algorithm**.

You probably remember that we mentioned and explained briefly hash functions in `Chapter 5`, *Five Forces of Bitcoin – #2 Cryptography*. We will discuss them again briefly, because they play such an important role in Proof-of-Work.

As we've already learned, a hash function can digest any kind of data, of any size, into a fixed length string of characters, which can serve as a unique digital fingerprint or identifier. Moreover, these cryptographic hash functions work only in one direction. Once we have the output, we cannot simply invert the function, plug in the output, and get the input data on the other end. This can be better described with the help of the following diagram:

To illustrate what it means to invert a function, let's consider the four basic mathematical operations:

- Addition and subtraction are inverse functions of each other
- Multiplication and division are inverse functions of each other

We can always construct equations with these functions to find any unknown variable. For example, $3 * x = 15$, $x = 15/3 = 5$.

Many mathematical functions can be inverted in a similar way. However, this is not the case with cryptographic hash functions. The only feasible way an unknown random variable can be found in a cryptographic function's input dataset is by trying different values for the unknown variable, one by one, given all the other known parameters, in order to find out what works. This is basically a brute-force approach of trying potentially all possible combinations. And this is precisely the element of work as used in Proof-of-Work. The work comprises all the iterative computations a computer needs to do to find the solution to the cryptographic puzzle.

Nonce and difficulty

Now, let's have a look again at the block header data examples we have. You may have noticed the word **Nonce** and another unfamiliar parameter called **Difficulty**.

The nonce is basically a random variable, or a source of randomness. Difficulty, on the other hand, is a temporary fixed number that is calculated by the Bitcoin protocol and remains fixed for approximately two weeks. We can see the two variables in the following example:

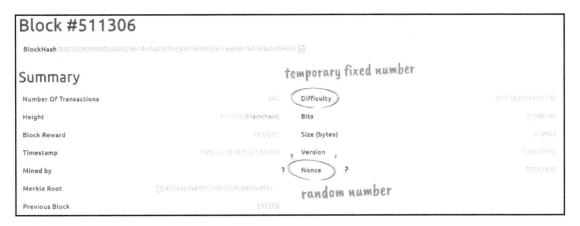

When a miner starts building or mining a block similar to this, all the parameters are known, except for the nonce. The nonce is the missing piece of the puzzle that needs to be found and plugged in, so that the resulting block header hash is less than a target difficulty level. You can think about target difficulty as a number. The process is done by trying different values for the nonce again and again in iterative calculations until a satisfactory hash is found.

Let's illustrate this with a straightforward example. Consider a game of dice, in which we have two players, throwing a couple of dice. The goal is to throw a number below or equal to a specific predetermined target number. The player who throws such a number first wins. If the target level is 10, the game is relatively easy, as only combinations summing up to 11 and 12 cannot win. All the other combinations win. Now, if we want to make the game more difficult, we can decrease the target to 5. In this case, a player needs to throw a dice sum of 2, 3, 4, or 5, in order to win. The odds of this are much lower compared to the previous target of 10, so the game is more difficult to win. If we want to make it really, really hard, we can reduce the target to 2 and then only a 1 and 1 combination of dice can win. The Bitcoin cryptographic computational puzzle works in a similar way.

You may be wondering why the block header hash should be less than the target difficulty level. Well, target difficulty is determined by the Bitcoin protocol based on the total amount of computer power plugged in and trying to solve the puzzle. As this is a random process, which follows a known statistical distribution, the odds of finding a nonce that solves the puzzle can be calculated in advanced. This means that the expected average time to find a solution of the puzzle by any node on the network, given the total processing power deployed, can also be calculated.

Target difficulty is adjusted by the system every 2,016 blocks, or approximately 2 weeks.

This is calculated by the Bitcoin software in such a way that the average time to mine a block stays around 10 minutes. This 10-minute block time was chosen as a reasonable compromise between speed and security of transactions on the blockchain.

The computing power

To give you an idea about the computer processing power mentioned here—it is defined as a hash rate or number of hash function calculations per unit of time. The most powerful Bitcoin mining chips currently can perform at a rate of 14 tera hash per second. This is 14 trillion hash function calculations per second! And a trillion is 1 with 12 zeros after it. A pretty large number, isn't it? You should also consider that these chips are designed specifically to optimize the calculation of this particular hash function and they cannot do anything else. They are called **ASICs**, which stands for **application-specific integrated circuits**.

Let's have a look at how difficulty has increased in line with the hash rate over time. The following screenshot depicts difficulty over time:

The hash rate over time is shown in the following screenshot:

To summarize, here are the key steps and takeaways from the mining process we covered so far:

1. Miners collect new transaction data broadcast on the network and verify it against a set of criteria, as per the Bitcoin protocols.
2. Then, miners order new verified transactions in blocks.
3. After that, miners prepare the new block header and calculate Proof-of-Work.
4. The first miner to find a solution to the Proof-of-Work puzzle (in other words, to compute a hash for the new block being mined), successfully mines this new block and includes it in the blockchain as the latest block.
5. The successful miner gets the block reward for the work done in terms of newly generated coins, which is known as the coinbase transaction.
6. The target difficulty for all miners on the network is adjusted by the protocol every 2,016 blocks, which is approximately 2 weeks, in order to maintain the average time between blocks of around 10 minutes. This adjustment is done in order to account for the amount of computer processing power deployed by miners on the network.
7. Thus, the more mining power is plugged in the system, the lower the bar is, making the problem more difficult to solve, but the average block time is kept at 10 minutes.

Next, we'll complete the puzzle of distributed consensus with some game theory.

Decentralized consensus and game theory

In this section, we will see how game theory comes into the picture.

Game theory is the study of mathematical models of conflict and cooperation between intelligent rational decision makers. It is mainly used in economics, political science, and psychology, as well as in logic and computer science.

Sounds exciting, doesn't it? Let's see how it applies to Bitcoin's decentralized consensus.

First, we need to consider that Bitcoin mining is a capital-intensive business. This means that miners need to make a large capital investment in expensive mining computer hardware, also known as **mining rigs**. Bitcoin mining is so industrialized nowadays that most of the hash power comes from large data centers, also called **mining pools**.

Besides capital expenses in physical hardware, there are also substantial operating expenses to run a mining operation. Such expenses include electricity for running the computers and for cooling them off. Remember that Bitcoin is a global transaction network that runs 24*7, so mining computers run Proof-of-Work calculations non-stop.

On top of that, there are property expenses for the physical location where miners store their computers, internet bandwidth, maintenance expenses, and other operating expenses.

All these investments and costs are effectively put at stake by the miners and are a huge economic incentive for them to act according to the Bitcoin protocol. This effectively guarantees the security of the decentralized consensus mechanism and the integrity of the blockchain.

You may wonder: why is this such a solid guarantee?

Bitcoin mining is a very competitive business. Miners compete based on their computer hash power to be the first to solve the Proof-of-Work puzzle, mine the next block, and get the block reward. It is so competitive that at present it is considered to be profitable only at places with very cheap electricity. A naturally cold climate is a great advantage too.

Considering all these factors, the best course of action for any miner is to follow the rules, verify transactions, and mine blocks in good faith. This gives miners the best chance to generate revenues from block rewards, thus realizing a return on their investment.

If a miner doesn't follow the protocol when mining a new block, such a block will not be accepted as valid by the other nodes on the network. This means no block rewards, and substantial economic losses for the delinquent miner.

Examples of miner misbehavior

Let's examine some scenarios of how a miner could potentially misbehave, and what follows on from that.

One such threat could be a miner who decides not to follow the rules for block rewards and tries to grab more coins in the coinbase transaction. According to the protocol, block rewards were 50 Bitcoin initially, with the issuing schedule halving every 4 years. So, currently it is 12.5 Bitcoin after it has halved twice since the launch of Bitcoin.

Consider a situation where a miner decides to try and reward himself or herself with 1,000 Bitcoin for mining a block, rather than 12.5, as per the protocol. Even if this greedy node successfully does the Proof-of-Work and comes up first with a solution to the cryptographic puzzle, the block will be rejected by the other nodes on the network. They will immediately spot the irregularity and will not accept this as a valid block.

You may wonder: how do they do this? How do the other nodes accept or reject a new candidate block?

First, they check whether all the criteria for valid blocks are met in accordance with the protocol. These include properly verified and recorded transactions, link to a previous block's hash, correct block reward, timestamp, and Proof-of-Work, among others.

If all is correct, but there are several valid candidate blocks or chains of blocks on the network at the same time, miners always choose to mine and build their new blocks on the longest chain. That is the chain with the most cumulative work done that goes back to the genesis block and the first transaction ever made by Satoshi. By selecting the parent block, which is the previous block in the chain, miners effectively vote with their mining power on the state of the blockchain. In this way, the original main valid chain is always extended, and more cumulative Proof-of-Work is added to it.

Each block mined on top of a given new block will count as one confirmation of this block and all transactions in it. The more blocks are built on top of a given block, the more confirmations this block has, and, therefore, the more secure and immutable all transactions in it are.

The block reward coins become spendable after 100 block confirmations. This is further protection embedded into the system to secure miners' integrity and to mitigate any risks of manipulation attempts by miners, such as changing the consensus rules, or double-spending.

Example of double-spending

What would happen if a miner tries to conspire and create double-spent transactions?

Imagine the following scenario. John wants to buy a car with Bitcoin. He finds a dealer of sports cars who accepts Bitcoin as a form of payment. John buys an awesome orange Lamborghini for 10 Bitcoin. Right after the payment is made and included in the blockchain as the top block, John drives away in his new Lambo. The vendor has delivered the product with no delay. However, John has colluded with Mr. Li who is a miner. Actually, Mr. Li operates a huge mining pool with a lot of processing power. Think about a big data center full of computers dedicated just to mining on the Bitcoin blockchain. Mr. Li immediately re-mines the same block containing John's payment to the car vendor, but this time the new re-mined block sends the same payment John made back to his wallet. This is double-spending! The same coins have been spent twice! John got the Lambo and his money back, so he got the Lambo for free! This situation can be better illustrated in the following diagram:

This situation creates a fork in the blockchain, meaning that two different blocks were mined at the same height of the blockchain. In other words, they were mined on top of the same parent block in a very close proximity. The next thing Mr. Li does is to continue mining on the chain containing the double-spent transaction to extend it and validate it further as the longest chain.

This kind of consensus attack is known as a 51% attack. Despite the name, it doesn't actually require 51% of the network hashing power; 51% is rather the threshold at which such an attack is almost guaranteed to succeed. This can be seen in the following diagram:

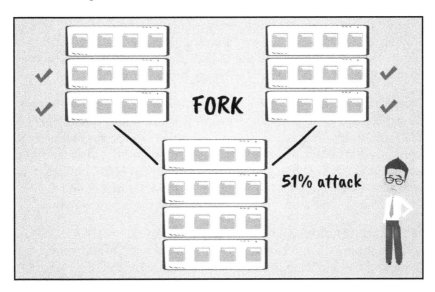

Such a scenario could be prevented easily if the vendor waits for more block confirmations before delivering the goods. Generally, after six block confirmations, a transaction is considered pretty much immutable. Therefore, it is recommended that large value purchases are delivered at least after six block confirmations, which is around 1 hour. Small-value purchases can be delivered faster because the risk of potential loss is smaller.

So, waiting for a sufficient number of block confirmations is one way to provide security against potential 51% attacks and double-spending.

The architecture surrounding the Bitcoin network

Another protection embedded in the system comes again from the miners' economic resources at stake. As we said, mining blocks and calculating Proof-of-Work consumes a lot of resources. If any miners decide to try to attack and take control of the network for their own benefit, this would be a very risky and expensive strategy. It would require an immense amount of computing power in order to succeed. We already mentioned the gigantic amount of hash power plugged in the Bitcoin network, so this is what any delinquent miners need to compete with, in order to tamper with the distributed ledger.

The more blocks are built on top of a given block, the more confirmations it has, and the harder it is to be manipulated. If any miners want to change a previous block, in order to create double-spent transactions, divert funds, or for any other reason, they would then need to re-mine all subsequent blocks. Moreover, all this work would be done basically for free, as they wouldn't earn any meaningful rewards on re-mined blocks. This is the case because their alternative chain would be competing with the original chain to become the longest and main chain of blocks. If not the longest, it would be ignored by the network, and no other miners would validate it by working on extending it.

Remember, miners always start building their new blocks on top of the longest existing chain, which contains the most cumulative Proof-of-Work done since the genesis block, the first block ever created. In this way, by linking each block to its parent block through hashes that contain all the block information, the entire network validates and confirms each and every transaction ever made on the blockchain. Every 10 minutes, when a new block is added to the blockchain, all transactions, right to the first one Satoshi made when he created Bitcoin, are re-validated and re-confirmed by the entire network.

Consider also that, while non-compliant nodes are re-mining past blocks, all the other honest nodes keep mining on and extending the original main blockchain. Therefore, the non-compliant nodes need to keep mining, at a faster rate than all the rest of the network, deploying more processing power and consuming more electricity, without any meaningful compensation.

The further back in time such an attack on the blockchain occurs, the lower the chance is that it would be feasible. And we are not talking years here, and not even months. We are talking weeks and days. There are 144 block confirmations in 24 hours. As we already mentioned, 100 block confirmations are required by the Bitcoin protocol for block reward coins to become spendable, so this is considered long enough to mitigate the risk of potential conflicts of interest for miners.

That's why it is so hard for an attacker to manipulate or take control over the Bitcoin blockchain. Now that the network has been live and up and running for almost a decade, the computing power plugged in mining, supporting the blockchain, and following the rules of the protocol, is enormous. This architecture probably makes it much more robust than any other payment network infrastructure that has ever existed.

Consensus attacks

It is important to mention one more thing about consensus attacks with regards to their potential impact. Such attacks can potentially disrupt the security of decentralized governance and availability of the network, but they cannot steal or spend other people's funds. This is because the only way to control funds on the blockchain is through private keys, which we covered in `Chapter 5`, *Five Forces of Bitcoin – #2 Cryptography*. Any potential consensus attackers can only manipulate their own transactions on the blockchain, and possibly create double-spent transactions with their own funds.

Now we've covered the decentralized consensus mechanism that provides security of the protocol by design. The Bitcoin blockchain architecture is incredibly effective and efficient in providing tamper-proof, censorship resistant track of records. It's hard to imagine a better accounting and record-keeping system, really.

Let's summarize all the factors in the Bitcoin mining and consensus process that we covered:

- Mining is highly competitive. Miners compete with their computational resources to mine blocks, satisfying the requirements of the decentralized consensus protocol.
- At each round of mining new blocks, the winner is the miner who is the first to find a solution to the Proof-of-Work puzzle in a valid block.
- The newly mined block is included in the blockchain by consensus expressed by all miners, who immediately start building their new candidate blocks on top of it. They do so by referencing its hash as a parent block to their new candidate blocks
- The winning miner gets the block reward, which currently stands at 12.5 Bitcoin.
- Security of the decentralized consensus mechanism is guaranteed by the miners' economic resources at stake, the Proof-of-Work algorithm, and the huge amount of hash power plugged in the network.

Summary

In this chapter, we learned all about consensus algorithms and how they came to be. We learned about the Byzantine Generals' Problem and how it is connected to the world of Bitcoin. We learned all about the Proof-of-Work algorithm that ensures the security and integrity of the Bitcoin protocol.

In the next chapter, we will get to know about the extensive peer-to-peer network that Bitcoin works on.

Five Forces of Bitcoin - #4 P2P Network

In this chapter, we will continue our journey through the world of Bitcoin. We'll cover the fourth force that powers Bitcoin—its **peer-to-peer** (**P2P**) network. We have covered cryptography, mining, blockchain, and many more features in the preceding chapters. Ever wondered how all these features work efficiently? This chapter will answer all your questions regarding the P2P network.

The following topics will be covered in this chapter:

- Introduction to P2P networks
- Nodes of the network
- Structure of the P2P network

Introduction to P2P networks

The web has become pretty centralized over the years with gigantic corporations holding enormous market power in e-commerce, web search, social networks, and many other areas. Besides market power, they control their users' private data too, such as identity information, credit card details, addresses, contact details, and so on. This is a very important privacy issue that users should pay attention to.

There are two types of approaches for network architecture of distributed applications:

- P2P model
- Client-server model

P2P model versus client-server model

The P2P and client-server models are two different approaches to address the network architecture of distributed applications. Distributed applications are systems whose components are located on different networked computers. These computers communicate and coordinate with each other over a network in order to run the distributed application.

The client-server model represents a centralized architecture where the server computer runs programs and shares its resources with client computers. Clients don't share any of their resources but send requests to the server for content, storage or processing:

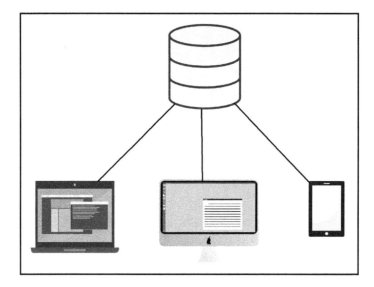

Examples of the client-server model include the email services, networked printing, and the World Wide Web.

On the other hand, P2P networks have no central server and each computer on the network shares its resources with the others. Such resources can include processing power, disk storage or network bandwidth. Interaction among peers is direct without the need for coordination by a central server. Peer network nodes are both consumers and suppliers of resources, as opposed to the client-server model where consumption and supply of resources are run separately. The architecture of P2P networks is as shown in the following diagram:

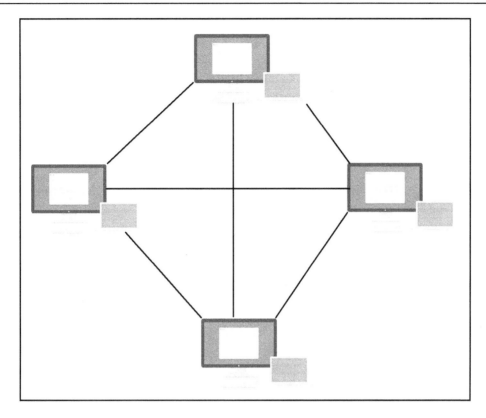

P2P systems gained popularity with the file sharing application Napster, which was released in 1999. Since then, the concept has evolved beyond the networks of peers doing similar things to systems with diverse peers bringing unique resources together to achieve superior results beyond the capabilities of individual peers. The original vision for the World Wide Web was close to a P2P network assuming that each user of the web would be an active editor and contributor, creating and linking content to form an interlinked web of links, but it has subsequently evolved to be dominated by the client-server model. The emergence of blockchain technology has given rise to the vision for Web 3.0, which should be based on more P2P interaction and decentralized services.

Financial transactions

Here's a tricky question for you. What are financial transactions nowadays?

The answer to that question would be that they are messages transmitted over a communication network. That's the way every bank transfer and credit card payment works. In fact, bank transfers are commonly referred to as **wire transfers**. You may have been wondering where this term comes from. Interestingly, it comes from telegraph networks, which are probably the oldest type of long-distance communication infrastructure. They transmit text messages over a wire. This is what Western Union started using in 1872 to transmit messages about payments. After a message with payment instructions was received at the destination, the local office made the payment to the designated person. That's how the concept of **wiring** money started.

This process has evolved through multiple steps until the present day, but at its core it continues to be based on transmitting messages. Financial networks are essentially communication networks.

How Bitcoin differs

Now, you may be thinking what's different and unique about the Bitcoin network compared to such financial networks?

The main difference is that Bitcoin is structured as a P2P network on top of the internet. Decentralization of control is a core design principle that is achieved and maintained by a flat P2P network architecture.

The Bitcoin P2P network is a collection of nodes or peers that run the Bitcoin protocol. The Bitcoin protocol is a piece of software engineering similar to the **Internet Protocol** (**IP**). Everyone has heard of IP addresses nowadays, which are used for communication over the internet. Just like the World Wide Web with its websites, domain names, and other applications, the Bitcoin network is a layer operating on top of the internet.

Bitcoin and other public blockchain network protocols can bypass the web. In fact, in some areas, they can provide a viable and superior alternative. Beyond payments, there are other game-changing blockchain applications, which we'll cover in detail later in Chapter 11, *Blockchains Focused on Specific Sectors and Use Cases*. The following are some of the areas where Bitcoin can be a viable alternative:

- E-commerce
- Web search
- Social networks
- ID authentication

Nodes of the Bitcoin network

Now, let's take a look at the various functions that participants on the Bitcoin network perform. These network peers (participants in the network) are referred to as nodes. All nodes can verify transactions, send their own transactions across the network, and keep a full or partial copy of the blockchain database.

In addition to the aforementioned functions, nodes on the network are sometimes involved with the mining function, which we discussed in Chapter 6, *Five Forces of Bitcoin – #3 Consensus Algorithm*. This involves calculating the Proof-of-Work algorithm and creating new blocks.

 Not all nodes on the Bitcoin network do mining, as it requires substantial resources and specialized equipment.

Types of nodes

It's important to distinguish between nodes that keep a full copy of the blockchain, referred to as **full nodes**, and nodes that keep only a partial copy, referred to as **lightweight nodes**, or **Simplified Payment Verification (SPV)** nodes.

Full nodes

Full nodes can autonomously verify transactions without external reference. They use a bottom-up verification approach. This means that they can track each and every coin from the moment of its creation through all transactions it's been involved in. In doing so, they start from the **genesis block** and go up the chain of blocks to get to the **current transaction** that needs to be verified. This can be better visualized using the following diagram:

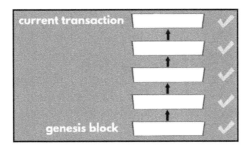

In this way, they know which coins have been spent and when, and who is the rightful owner of each coin at all times. Maintaining a full node comes with its own resource requirements in terms of storage capacity, as the size of the Bitcoin blockchain currently stands at 160 gigabytes.

SPV nodes

Alternatively, nodes can store only a part of the blockchain and still be able to verify transactions. Such nodes are called lightweight nodes and they use SPV. This is a top-down approach.

SPV nodes keep just the block headers of all blocks, which takes a small fraction of the storage space required for the full blockchain. To verify a transaction, they check the blocks to find out where the specific transaction belongs and then make sure there are at least six blocks built on top of that block. In this way, lightweight nodes rely on the work done by full nodes as a proof that the transaction being verified is in order and has not been double spent. Lightweight nodes effectively verify transactions by checking the Proof-of-Work in the chain of blocks these transactions belong to. Many Bitcoin wallets, especially those on smartphones, are lightweight nodes. The process can be further illustrated using the following diagram:

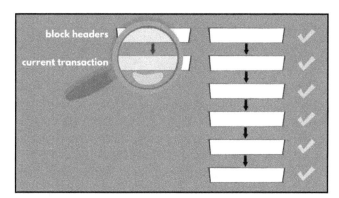

The Bitcoin P2P network

The Bitcoin P2P network contains a vast array of nodes spread all over the internet working in tandem. There are two main parts of the Bitcoin network:

- The mainnet
- The testnet

The mainnet

The mainnet is the core Bitcoin network hosted on the internet where all the real-life transactions take place. All the Bitcoin activity that we see on the internet occurs on the mainnet.

The mainnet contains all the vital information that's used in Bitcoin transactions around the world. So, a question you might be asking yourself is what if there is some new upgrade? How will it affect the Bitcoin network? The solution to this question is the testnet.

The testnet

Besides the main Bitcoin network, called the mainnet, there is also a testnet where new projects and protocol features are tested. The testnet is an alternative blockchain used for testing and research. The testnet is a security measure to ensure that the main Bitcoin network is never jeopardized in the process of experimentation. In this network, we use Testnet coins.

Testnet coins are separate and distinct from the actual mainnet Bitcoins. They aren't supposed to have any value. This allows application developers or testers to experiment, without having to use real Bitcoins or putting the main blockchain at risk of faulty software.

Additional entities

In addition to the main Bitcoin network, there are other entities running full nodes to interface with the mainnet. Such entities provide specific services to the network. The following are some of the entities used:

- **Mining pools**: Mining pools can be structured as a server running a full node, and many other computers will be connected to it and running Proof-of-Work calculations, but without needing to store the full blockchain.
- **Exchanges**: Exchanges are places where Bitcoin and other cryptocurrencies are traded on a daily basis.
- **Blockchain explorers**: Blockchain explorers are basically search engines for blockchain transactions.

Summary

In this chapter, we learned that Bitcoin is the first ever implementation of a decentralized P2P network for payments and value transfers. The system works smoothly and efficiently without any need for third-party interference. We learned about decentralization of control, the different types of nodes in the Bitcoin network, and the structure of the Bitcoin network.

In the next chapter, we will learn about the software code base that powers Bitcoin.

Five Forces of Bitcoin - #5 Software Code Base

8

In this chapter, we'll check out the last and probably the most core part of Bitcoin—its software code base. In this chapter, we'll focus on the software side of things. We will learn about the protocols and functions that help Bitcoin function seamlessly. The following topics will be covered in this chapter:

- Introduction to Bitcoin's software code case
- Bitcoin's scripting language
- Bitcoin as an application platform

Introduction to Bitcoin's software code case

As we all know by now, the Bitcoin ecosystem consists of users, miners, software developers, and applications, such as exchanges, wallets, and blockchain explorers. Other stakeholders are expected to get increasingly involved as well. It is highly likely that regulators and government agencies will pay more attention to the ecosystem in future. The following diagram represents the Bitcoin ecosystem:

All participants in the Bitcoin network run software, which is developed and maintained by software engineers.

Bitcoin was first developed as a software protocol by Satoshi Nakamoto, who produced the initial code base. Shortly after the launch, Satoshi passed on the continued development and maintenance of the code to a group of software development enthusiasts who embraced the idea. This initial group has evolved into the core development team of Bitcoin. That said, Bitcoin is an open source project, and everyone can review the code and contribute with development proposals.

Bitcoin Core is the open source software code base that powers Bitcoin. It is known as the reference implementation of Bitcoin, meaning that it is the main point of reference of how the Bitcoin system functions. It determines all aspects of the system, such as wallets, transactions, block validation, node setup, and network protocol in the peer-to-peer network.

Now, we will move on to the key software applications used in the ecosystem.

Wallets

Wallets containing users' private keys are the tools necessary to store funds and make transactions on the blockchain. They are the most common user interface to the Bitcoin system. In a way, this is similar to web browsers being the most common user interface to the World Wide Web and its **HyperText Transfer Protocol** (**HTTP**) protocol.

All wallets contain cryptographic keys, giving access to coins on the blockchain. We covered cryptographic keys in detail in `Chapter 5`, *Five Forces of Bitcoin – #2 Cryptography*. Wallets can be divided into several types, depending on the way they store and manage keys:

- We can have desktop wallets, representing software applications installed and run on PCs and laptops
- We can also have mobile wallets, which are mobile applications installed on smartphones
- In addition, there are web wallets, which are accessed through a web browser. These wallets are stored on a third-party server, similar to some email account services, such as Gmail

Besides these software wallet applications, we can also have some wallets that are not software-based. These are hardware wallets and paper wallets:

- Hardware wallets are specialized hardware devices designed to securely store private keys. In their appearance, they are similar to USB sticks
- Paper wallets, on the other hand, are a surprisingly low-tech but highly effective solution against potential hacking attacks, as they simply store cryptographic keys on paper. Of course, such paper wallets must be securely physically stored to mitigate the risk of theft

Wallets that store keys offline are also known as cold storage.

We'll repeat this here again, as it is so important to remember: whoever controls the private keys, controls the funds on the blockchain, so any wallets must be managed, secured, and backed up with the greatest diligence.

Wallets can be part of a full node that stores the entire blockchain, or a lightweight node that only stores its own transactions. Lightweight nodes rely on full nodes they connect to, in order to access the complete Bitcoin blockchain.

Blockchain explorer

Besides wallets, another commonly used software application is a blockchain explorer. A blockchain explorer is a tool used as a search engine for the blockchain. It allows us to track transactions, blocks, and address balances. In a way, this is similar to what Google Search does on the web.

There are several sites that act as blockchain explorers. One of the most frequently used explorer sites is `blockchain.info`. The following screenshot contains a quick preview of the blockchain explorer:

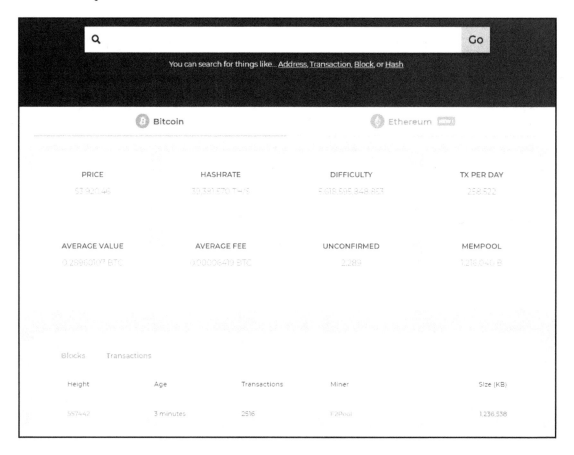

Bitcoin's scripting language

Now, let's have a look at the programmability aspect of Bitcoin. Some blockchain cryptocurrencies are referred to as programmable money.

Bitcoin is indeed a programmable digital currency. It uses a programming language called Script in structuring and processing transactions. As the name suggests, this is a script type of language, which supports small programs called scripts. They automate the execution of a list of tasks, or commands, that otherwise could be executed one-by-one manually by a human operator.

Script is a high-level programming language with limited functionality, which is also domain-specific, meaning it's specialized to its application domain. Bitcoin's transaction script was specifically designed to be limited in scope, in order to require minimal processing and to be executable even on very simple devices. Its limited scope also enhances security because this leaves less space for coding errors. As you can imagine, any errors in a system processing money transfers can be quite costly.

Script is not a Turing-complete language, meaning that it is not general-purpose and cannot be used for programs solving just any problem. We'll talk more about Turing completeness when we discuss Ethereum in the coming chapters.

Bitcoin's transaction script includes functions that drive transaction execution. Each transaction script has the following steps:

1. When a sender signs a transaction with a cryptographic key, the script locks the coins being sent, which are basically transaction inputs.
2. These coins or transaction inputs can then be unlocked only by the receiver's private key.
3. After that, the coins in the form of transaction outputs are transferred to the receiver's account and are controlled by the receiver's private key. Given these two steps of each Bitcoin transaction, the most common scripts used to validate transactions are a locking script and an unlocking script.

This is better illustrated in the following diagram:

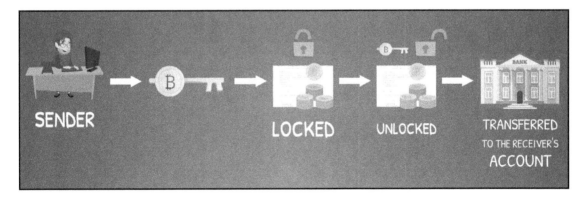

Bitcoin transaction scripts can also be a bit more complex, involving several conditions to unlock coins or transaction outputs. In this way, it becomes possible to structure multi-signature transactions requiring more than one private key to unlock the coins. This can be used to send money to multiple receivers in one transaction or to send money to an entity with multiple stakeholders who have joint control over the funds. For instance, a company with several partners, which receives Bitcoin may find multi-signature transactions a useful way to manage such transfers.

Another useful feature for transaction structuring are time locks. Time-bound conditions can be included in a script, so that funds are unlocked at a specific time or after a specific period of time following an event.

There are other useful logical conditions that can be included in Bitcoin transaction scripts. These include conditional clauses, such as IF...THEN...ELSE. You are probably familiar with the IF and other conditional functions, if you have used spreadsheet software, such as Excel, or studied any type of programming. The purpose and effect of such clauses in a Bitcoin script are similar. The funds are unlocked only if certain conditions are present.

The various programming features of the Bitcoin script language can be combined together to produce more complex conditional transactions than a simple payment. For example, the escrow account type of transaction structures can be programmed and automated with Bitcoin scripts.

Traditional escrow accounts are typically created when two parties agree to a payment, but only if certain conditions have been met. The payer creates an escrow account with a respected third party (traditionally a bank) and transfers the funds to the escrow account. Once the necessary condition has been met, and the third party is able to verify that happened, it transfers the money to the intended recipient.

In Bitcoin, payment conditions can be programmed to automatically execute a transaction without any need for a third-party agent.

This logic and functionality is the basis for the smart contracts, which you may have heard of. We'll discuss smart contracts in more detail when we examine Ethereum, which takes smart contracts to the next level.

Bitcoin as an application platform

There is another way we can look at Bitcoin—as an application platform.

The key features of the Bitcoin blockchain, such as programmability, transparency, immutability, integrity, accountability, auditability, decentralized consensus, timestamping, security, direct peer-to-peer interaction, and its open source nature, among others, can enable a large range of applications beyond payments.

Bitcoin was originally designed as a payment system, but the baseline technologies that power it and its architecture open up much broader use cases. Its building blocks are not accounts, balances, payments, and wallets. This is rather a user-friendly application interface. In a similar way, other use cases and applications can be built on the Bitcoin blockchain.

Let's have a look at a few examples.

Asset registry

Digital notary and asset registers, the blockchain properties of Bitcoin, make it a perfect system for demonstrating proof of ownership. Blockchain technology can be a suitable and efficient solution for real estate property registers, shareholder registers, and other investment securities registers. It can be used to register the ownership and transfers of any kind of asset or property rights, including intangible property, such as trademarks, and intellectual property. Such implementations can be realized through separate dedicated blockchains, but the Bitcoin blockchain can be used as well.

The Bitcoin blockchain has some clear advantages over any alternative blockchains—it is the most secure, the most immutable, and decentralized one. This is the case because it is the first and foremost successfully operating public blockchain and has the largest pool of computing resources securing its decentralized consensus system. In this way, assets external to the blockchain can be digitalized and traded on it, in addition to intrinsic assets, such as Bitcoins.

Trade finance and crowdfunding campaigns are another possible use case for Bitcoin. Such applications are enabled by escrow, programmability, and smart contract functionality of a blockchain. Transaction scripts can be structured, so funds are released under certain conditions that can be time-bound or depending on achieving certain milestones.

Imagine that a retailer in Europe wants to import and sell merchandise from China (for example, consumer electronics, such as TVs, refrigerators, microwaves, and so on). The retailer orders the merchandise from the manufacturer, which then needs to be loaded on a cargo ship and sent to Europe. Both parties to this transaction need security and assurance that they will get what they expect out of it. Travel times for ships to deliver goods from China to Europe are around 1 month. This raises counterparty risk that one of the parties may not receive its fair share of the value exchange. From the perspective of the vendor (in this case, the Chinese manufacturer), they need to be confident that they will get paid, before they load the merchandise on the ship, because at this point shipping costs start getting incurred. The merchandise is also at risk of being stolen or otherwise compromised, while in transit. From the perspective of the buyer, the European retailer company, they need to be confident they will receive the merchandise safe and sound before they release the payment to the vendor.

This type of international trade transaction is currently managed by a trusted third party, such as a bank. International banks offer trade finance services, such as escrow accounts and letters of credit. The way this system works currently is that the buyer deposits the funds for the payment to the vendor in an escrow account held at a bank. The bank then issues a letter of credit to the vendor, guaranteeing the funds are there and will be released upon successful delivery and receipt of the goods. This is summarized in the following diagram:

You can probably see how this process can be automated with a single smart contract on the blockchain. This new technological paradigm will render such transactions much cheaper and more efficient. A single technological interface will facilitate direct interaction between buyers and sellers, thus eliminating any potential rent-seeking behavior by intermediaries acting as gate-keepers. Moreover, this interface can be a public, open source technology, such as the Bitcoin blockchain, which is not controlled or owned by any single third party.

Crowdfunding

The crowdfunding use case can be enabled by smart contracts releasing funds to the project being funded upon reaching certain milestones or targets. This can be a viable decentralized alternative to Kickstarter or other existing start-up funding platforms. Again, the Bitcoin blockchain can provide the transaction protocol infrastructure to implement such solutions as a second-layer technology and user interfaces on top of it.

These are not just hypothetical use cases and applications. There are projects that have been developing such solutions already for a few years. One such application is called **colored coins**. The term comes from marking or coloring a nominal amount of Bitcoin to represent something more than the amount of digital currency itself. Colored coins can serve as a certificate of ownership of any kind of asset, commodity, or property, as we discussed. They use the Bitcoin transaction scripts to encode and store additional data related to such other assets or properties. This additional data is called **metadata**. When colored coins are created or issued by inserting the relevant piece of code in a Bitcoin transaction, this registers the external asset on the Bitcoin blockchain and creates an asset ID with a timestamp. When such colored coins are transacted on the Bitcoin blockchain, this effectively transfers the value and ownership of the external assets associated with the colored coins.

Another similar project is the Counterparty protocol. It is a secondary protocol layer built on top of Bitcoin. Similar to colored coins, it enables digitalization of ownership rights and transfer of any kind of external assets. It also features a decentralized asset exchange and smart contracts. The Counterparty protocol, in turn, can serve as a platform for other applications to be built on top of it, using its additional functionality and the security of the underlying Bitcoin blockchain.

Summary

We have reached the end of this chapter! Now, you should be able to appreciate what a unique system Bitcoin is. It is the first and foremost implementation of a decentralized digital currency and peer-to-peer payment system. To recap, the five powers powering Bitcoin are as follows:

- Blockchain
- Cryptography
- Proof-of-Work consensus algorithm
- P2P network
- Software code base

All these create powerful network effects and are further reinforced with the growth of the Bitcoin community and ecosystem. With increased user adoption, more applications and use cases, the value of the network grows, which in turn creates incentives for further development and innovation leading to an even higher future growth potential.

We started our Bitcoin journey from the roots of the technology and reviewed its successful launch and evolution. We went on to examine more sophisticated concepts and related applications, such as smart contracts and digital property rights. We can refer to Bitcoin as Blockchain 1.0, as it is the first generation of this technology and it started this new industrial revolution.

Now, it's time to move on and see what Ethereum is all about.

How Ethereum Took the Idea of Blockchain to the Next Level

9

Now that you already understand how each of the five forces shaping Bitcoin's technology work, we are ready to introduce Ethereum, the first Turing-complete blockchain platform. If you are not completely sure what Turing-complete means just yet, don't worry, we'll cover it in this chapter.

The following topics will be covered in this chapter:

- Introduction to Ethereum
- How Ethereum came into existence
- Understanding Ethereum
- The Ethereum Virtual Machine

Introduction to Ethereum

As we mentioned in the previous chapters, Bitcoin planted the seed of blockchain technology and cryptoassets, and quickly started gathering a passionate and dedicated community of enthusiasts and supporters. A new movement was set in motion by the ingenious system Satoshi created. The momentum accelerated at an exponential rate and generated a snowball effect of innovation. Further technological disruption and breakthroughs in the blockchain space were imminent. These effects were reinforced by the open source nature of Bitcoin.

Many developers started experimenting with the Bitcoin code by creating alternative cryptoasset protocols. Such new alternative blockchains came to be referred as **altcoins** (given that they are an alternative to the original coin, Bitcoin). The following diagram shows the evolution of Bitcoin:

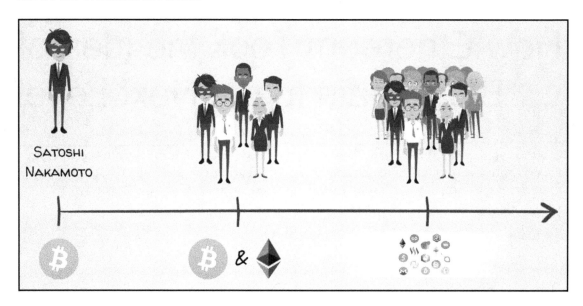

By far the greatest impact and most significant innovation in this new space has come with Ethereum. That's why we'll cover it extensively here.

Ethereum represents the second generation of blockchain technology with enhanced functionality beyond payments and distributed asset ledgers. One of its key domain areas is decentralized computing. The vision of Ethereum's founder, Vitalik Buterin, was to create a decentralized global computer, which was implemented through the **Ethereum Virtual Machine (EVM)**.

Ethereum works based on the same fundamental principles and technologies underpinning Bitcoin:

- Blockchain
- Cryptography
- Proof-of-Work consensus algorithm
- Peer-to-peer network
- Software code base

The key innovation, which differentiates Ethereum from Bitcoin and many other altcoins, is its Turing-complete programming language. Turing-complete means that Ethereum's programming language can be used to program and run pretty much any function or task. This enables a broader range of decentralized applications to be created and deployed. It packs a complete set of tools for developers to innovate further and build applications and businesses on the blockchain. The Ethereum blockchain serves as a backbone infrastructure for an entire economic and social ecosystem. That's why the majority of **decentralized blockchain applications** (or **DAPPs** for short), at the moment, use the Ethereum platform.

As we will see later, the downside of such larger code base is a larger attack surface and risk of software bugs, which will occur inevitably.

Let's take it step-by-step, and see how Ethereum has evolved since its inception.

How Ethereum came into existence

The idea of Ethereum was conceived in 2013 by Vitalik Buterin who was 19 years old at the time. Vitalik was drawn into computer games initially, similar to many of his peers. His father, also a computer scientist, introduced him to Bitcoin, which Vitalik embraced and started exploring with enthusiasm. He co-founded Bitcoin Magazine in 2011 and worked as a journalist there. He also collaborated on colored coin projects. You probably remember colored coins, which we covered in detail in the previous chapter about Bitcoin. They enable basic implementations of smart contracts and digital assets on the Bitcoin blockchain. Vitalik wanted to expand the concept of colored coins to enable larger, more flexible and powerful applications to run on the blockchain. When he faced resistance to his idea from Bitcoin core developers, he decided to launch his own project and to design it from scratch.

Vitalik is a prolific blockchain thought leader. His talent was recognized even before Ethereum achieved global success. At a very young age, he was placed in a class for gifted children. He won a bronze model at the International Olympiad in Informatics in 2012 at the age of 18. In 2013, he wrote the Ethereum whitepaper outlining his vision.

In 2014, Vitalik received the World Technology Award for IT software, along with other distinguished winners such as Elon Musk who received the award for Energy.

Also in 2014, he received the prestigious Thiel Fellowship and dropped out of the University of Waterloo, to focus on Ethereum full-time.

The Theil fellowship

The Thiel fellowship was created by the billionaire entrepreneur and investor Peter Thiel, who co-founded PayPal and Palantir, both of which became multi-billion dollar companies. He is a prominent venture capitalist and was the first outside investor in Facebook. With his fellowship, Peter Thiel aims to sponsor talented young people under the age of 23, who leave the traditional path of college to pursue projects with a high global impact. Such projects can include scientific research, start-ups, or social enterprises. With less than 1% selection rate, the award is considered more competitive than gaining acceptance to the world's best universities.

Having some funding from Thiel, Vitalik went on to gather a talented team of co-founders and developers, and to pursue his vision for Ethereum. And oh boy, was this a grand vision! The team wanted to create Web 3.0, a more decentralized and smarter next generation of the Internet, powered by Ethereum.

Since they needed more funding, the founders launched an **Initial Coin Offering** (**ICO**) in July 2014, which was effectively a presale of ether, the native cryptoasset of the future Ethereum platform. They managed to raise around $18m dollars' worth of Vitcoin, which was the currency they accepted for contributions, and this represented the largest ICO at the time. This form of start-up capital raising through crowdsourcing was about to experience widespread adoption and parabolic growth over the next years. We'll talk more about ICOs later on.

With sufficient funding secured, the founding team had many months of hard work ahead of them, until the Ethereum network went live in July 2015.

Let's get into it—welcome to Blockchain 2.0.

Understanding Ethereum

If we want to understand Ethereum, probably the best starting point is to have a look at its whitepaper. So, let's see how its founders describe it, shall we?

The Ethereum whitepaper starts as follows:

*"Satoshi Nakamoto's development of Bitcoin in 2009 has often been hailed as a radical development in money and currency, being the first example of a digital asset, which simultaneously has no backing or "intrinsic value" and no centralized issuer or controller. However, another, arguably more important, part of the Bitcoin experiment is the underlying blockchain technology as a tool of distributed consensus, and attention is rapidly starting to shift to this other aspect of Bitcoin. Commonly cited alternative applications of blockchain technology include using on-blockchain digital assets to represent custom currencies and financial instruments (colored coins), the ownership of an underlying physical device (smart property), non-fungible assets such as domain names (Namecoin), as well as more complex applications involving having digital assets being directly controlled by a piece of code implementing arbitrary rules (smart contracts) or even blockchain-based **decentralized autonomous organizations** (**DAOs**). What Ethereum intends to provide is a blockchain with a built-in fully fledged Turing-complete programming language that can be used to create contracts that can be used to encode arbitrary state transition functions, allowing users to create any of the systems described here, as well as many others that we have not yet imagined, simply by writing up the logic in a few lines of code."*

What the whitepaper tells us, is that blockchain technology has many potential use cases beyond payments. Ethereum takes the technology a step further innovating upon the pioneer in the space, Bitcoin. A very ambitious plan, isn't it?

Ethereum provides the tools to facilitate the creation of custom digital assets, financial instruments, and decentralized applications. Everyone can launch their own project and create a digital asset, a DAPP, or an entire DAO using the open source Ethereum protocol.

Digital assets on the blockchain are referred to as **smart property**, meaning that any physical asset such as gold, real estate, stocks, bonds, art, and so on, can be represented by a token, and stored or transacted on a distributed ledger.

In addition, smart contracts enable complex financial instruments and applications to be created. In this way, smart property can be included in smart contracts and transacted under certain conditions programmed in the contract. Remember our trade finance example from the Bitcoin chapter where a smart contract can substitute an escrow account and a letter of credit provided by a bank? In transactions where product delivery takes time, a smart contract can be set up, so it releases the funds to the vendor upon successful delivery of the goods to the buyer.

Combining smart property and smart contracts could lead to DAOs where the business logic of operating an entire organization is programmed in a complex system of smart contracts. For now, it remains to be seen how this would work in practice.

As mentioned previously, these ideas have been explored by various projects before Ethereum. However, previous projects were using Bitcoin and other blockchain protocols less suitable for the purpose, while Ethereum is specifically designed for this.

The Ethereum protocol and its development team do not directly create or support decentralized applications, but they provide the tools, building blocks, and infrastructure for developers to launch them. Ethereum takes the concept of a blockchain beyond cryptocurrency in an innovative and meaningful way.

Next, we'll have a closer look at some of the key elements of Ethereum.

The Ethereum Virtual Machine

At this point you are probably thinking—OMG! Another virtual thing! We had to get used to abstractions such as virtual currencies, virtual assets and now we are talking about virtual machines?! Well, we live in the digital information age, so virtual goods and virtual reality are going to be more and more present in our everyday life. So, it's useful to get comfortable with such concepts step-by-step. Virtual machines are a pretty abstract concept, so we'll try and tackle the difficult task of explaining it from several angles.

Introduction to virtual machines

Virtual machines are not an entirely new idea in distributed computing. With the continued development of the World Wide Web, the number of software products and services migrating in the cloud has been steadily increasing. Business models and information infrastructure have evolved and adapted to the new paradigm of the web. It is more effective and efficient to share and distribute computing resources, rather than store and process everything on the same computer. An example of this is shown in the following diagram:

The concept of cloud computing and virtualization is based on the separation between the different components of a computer system. At the top level, we have hardware and software. Then, we can break down the different types of software into additional layers, such as software operating systems and software applications.

A virtual machine is another construct that comes on top of computer hardware, or a standard operating system such as Windows, and interacts with various applications. A virtual machine basically creates a virtual operating system environment that can be separated from the hardware. Just as any other virtual machine in a network, it is isolated from a network yet it is a part of the network.

This isolation from the network is what makes it invulnerable to hack threats or any data corruption. This allows an entire operating system to be copied and pasted from one hardware device to another, just as any other file (similar to a video, a picture, or a text file). Such virtualization is part of cloud computing, which is so popular nowadays. The following diagram shows the architecture of the virtual machine:

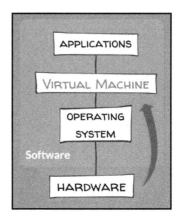

As seen in the preceding diagram, the **operating system** (**OS**) and its applications share hardware resources from a single host server, or from a pool of host servers. Each virtual machine requires its own underlying OS, and the hardware is virtualized. A hypervisor, or a virtual machine monitor, is software, firmware, or hardware that creates and runs virtual machines. It sits between the hardware and the virtual machine and is necessary to virtualize the server.

Many software products and services are increasingly being delivered on-demand, on the cloud, which means they are internet-based and distributed. Microsoft Office with its Word, Excel, and PowerPoint applications, which have become pretty much a software household name and office staple of the 1990s and early 2000s, now have their cloud-based alternatives, such as Google Docs, Google Sheets, and Google Slides.

More and more businesses and consumers are turning to cloud-based solutions.

Salesforce.com Inc. is another popular **software as a service** (**SaaS**) company, which delivers **customer relationship management** (**CRM**) and other enterprise software services on the cloud. It led the way with its new business model and started competing with traditional enterprise software giants such as Oracle and SAP. Given how disruptive and effective cloud computing is, all the established industry leaders soon followed suit with their own cloud solutions.

This migration towards web-based services was enabled to a large extent by the advent of the Java programming language and the **Java virtual machine** (**JVM**). That's because they made it easier to create large scale web applications. Applications written in Java can run on any JVM, regardless of underlying computer system architectures.

Ethereum introduced the virtual machine concept to the blockchain world. The EVM enables standardized smart contracts and decentralized applications to be created and run on the blockchain. This is done with the help of a Turing-complete programming language, such as Solidity, which was purposely designed by the Ethereum development team. Turing-complete means that it is general purpose or computationally universal, in other words it can be used to program and perform pretty much any function or task. This design makes Ethereum a perfectly suitable environment for decentralized applications. The following diagram shows how EVMs would function in conjunction:

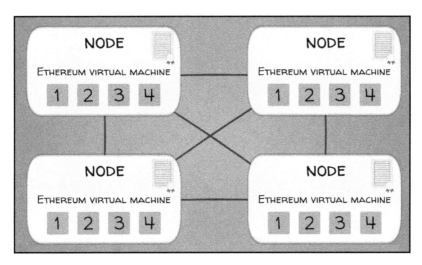

For example, consider security in EVMs. Hackers are really stubborn, and they have attempted breaking through the blockchain platforms trying to steal the cryptocurrencies. They have been successful recently with a few others, but not with Ethereum platform, because of the EVM, as it has become the platform's shield against the hackers, making hacking into an Ethereum platform very difficult. For securing the platforms, the EVM tends to secure firewalls of the platform, and reinforces security measures. This ensures the safety of the tokens and transactions that are present on the system encrypted.

We can extrapolate now a long-term trend in technology, from the original software applications companies such as Microsoft and Oracle launched back in the 70s and 80s, to the cloud-based but still centralized services companies such as Google and Salesforce pioneered in the late 90s and early 2000s, to the decentralized applications of the future. Blockchain-based decentralized applications could become the next big thing in computer technology, which will complement and compete with the currently available cloud solutions. We'll cover that in more detail in the following chapters.

Summary

In this chapter, we learned all about Ethereum and how it revolutionalized the internet. We learnt how Ethereum was invented and why. We also learned how Ethereum functions using EVMs to create decentralized applications.

We learned about the wide range of smart contracts and decentralized applications powered by EVMs. In the following chapters, we'll focus on some of the key innovations Ethereum has brought to the world.

10
Ethereum - A Global Platform for Decentralized Applications

In this chapter, we'll discuss Ethereum, which we call Blockchain 2.0. As you'll soon find out, Ethereum takes smart contracts and smart assets to a whole new level with its complete and flexible programming language. This opens up an even broader range of opportunities and futuristic concepts, such as decentralized autonomous organizations, which can potentially be managed automatically without much human involvement. That said, the underlying blockchain architecture still remains similar to that of Bitcoin. This highlights the proven technological breakthroughs and foundational importance of the Bitcoin blockchain.

Nevertheless, the blockchain space is undergoing heavy development and continued innovation, so we should expect more interesting projects to come. The following topics will be covered in this chapter:

- Decentralized applications based on Ethereum
- How Ethereum works
- Decentralized autonomous organizations

Decentralized applications based on Ethereum

We already learned that Bitcoin is the first public blockchain system designed for peer-to-peer payments. It is the pre-eminent cryptoasset.

Ethereum took blockchain technology a step further aiming to become a global decentralized computing platform. It started the second generation of public blockchain technology. The goal of Ethereum is ambitious and enterprising: it aims to enable a large ecosystem of decentralized applications on the blockchain, and thus create a more decentralized version of the World Wide Web—a project known as **Web 3.0**.

OK! So, what would these decentralized applications look like?

Types of decentralized applications

We can broadly distinguish three main types of applications outlined in the Ethereum white paper.

The first type is purely financial applications that provide complex financial products and solutions through smart contracts. These can include insurance, financial derivatives, escrow accounts for trade settlement, financial trusts, and crowdfunding. A good example for this type of applications comes from a company called Etherisc, which is developing insurance policies based on Ethereum smart contracts. They have a working product for flight insurance, which provides automatic premium pay-off to passengers in case of a delayed or cancelled flight. This solution brings a clear advantage to customers as they get their premium paid off automatically, with no delay, once a coverage trigger event occurs. Typically, getting a refund for a delayed or cancelled flight has been a cumbersome and lengthy process plagued by bureaucracy, which can drag on for months or even years. And we all know how often flights have issues with being on time. Therefore, Etherisc brings a clear and compelling value proposition to customers, who generally aren't treated fairly by airlines and traditional insurance companies alike. This new solution is powered by Ethereum.

You can see the business logic of Etherisc's insurance smart contract in the following diagram:

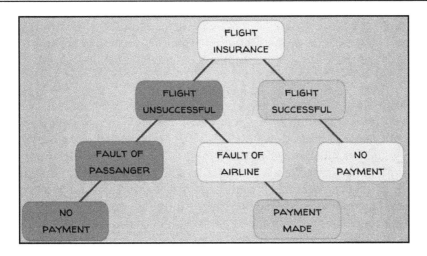

Another major category of applications is ones with some sort of financial angle, perhaps involving the use of money on the platform, but that also have a substantial non-monetary component. They can be used in gaming, betting, prediction markets, and any decentralized peer-to-peer marketplaces for products or services. One such application based on Ethereum is Fun Fair. It provides turnkey online casino technology that can be used as a white label solution by anyone, anywhere to create an online casino. With the help of blockchain and smart contracts, Fun Fair brings transparency, security, and efficiency to both players and online casino operators:

With regards to peer-to-peer marketplaces, some primary use cases include decentralized data storage, computing, web hosting, electricity trading, and media and content distribution platforms. Pretty much any type of resource and market you can think of can benefit from a peer-to-peer sharing economy.

For example, projects such as Golem and SONM are building decentralized marketplaces for spare computing power based on Ethereum. Their vision is to enable the sharing and trading of unused computer processing capacity by participants on their distributed platforms.

The concept is similar to the sharing economy Airbnb creates with its platform for renting out underutilized real estate. In this way, **Golem** and **SONM** aim to create a worldwide supercomputer network that employs idle PCs all over the planet. Excess computing power can be used by scientists, businesses, or consumers that need to run large amounts of computation, while providers of such resources can be rewarded. All transactions are automated with smart contracts and benefit from direct and decentralized peer-to-peer interaction, thus maximizing the value for users. All this economic activity benefits from the security and programmability of the Ethereum blockchain. The following diagram shows the flow of Golem:

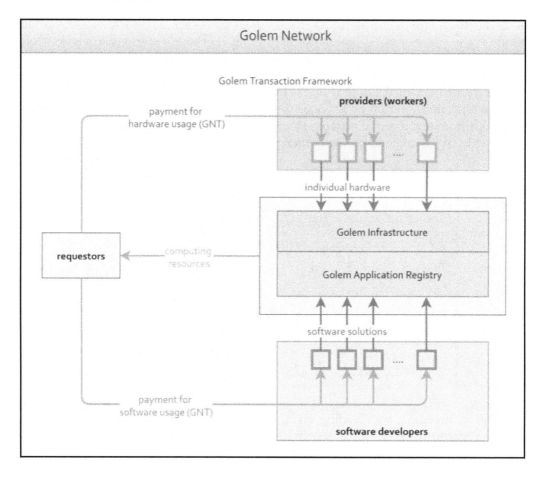

Following a similar logic, Power Ledger and WePower are building decentralized peer-to-peer platforms for electricity trading and the funding of renewable energy projects. Both platforms run on Ethereum.

Another interesting project, **Substratum** is building a decentralized censorship-resistant peer-to-peer web-hosting platform based on Ethereum. This platform tackles the important global problems of cybersecurity and net neutrality. Net neutrality is the principle that all data on the internet should be treated fairly and equally by **internet service providers** (**ISP**). Here again, providers of spare computer resources for web hosting get rewarded via transactions on the blockchain.

Another interesting example comes from **Basic Attention Token** (**BAT**). This project introduces an innovative concept for the advertising industry with its decentralized advertising marketplace. It proposes a superior economic model for all parties involved – advertisers, publishers, *and* consumers. The project is led by Brendan Eich, the creator of the JavaScript programming language and co-founder of Mozilla Firefox, the popular web browser. This solution uses smart contracts on the Ethereum blockchain to tokenize and trade consumer attention to online ads, just like any other commodity. The BAT platform uses its native tokens and smart contracts to distribute value across the advertising ecosystem. The Brave browser is an integral part of this system – it blocks third-party ads and trackers, and measures user attention to online content using embedded and transparent machine learning algorithms. User profiles are protected by anonymity protocols and features but still provide useful data for targeted ads on the platform. Users get rewarded for their attention with native tokens; in other words, they get paid to view ads. This is a completely disruptive concept as, so far, there hasn't been a reward mechanism for consumers to monetize their attention to ads. There are no middlemen on the platform, such as data brokers, which typically collect personal information, aggregate it, build consumer profiles, and sell this to advertisers, thereby monetizing people's personal data. Cutting out such middlemen creates efficiencies and value for consumers, publishers, and advertisers alike. BAT's smart contracts automatically distribute the flow of value in the ecosystem as follows: advertisers send payments in native tokens along with ads to users, as users view ads, the smart contracts unlock the funds and send payments to the users, the Brave platform, and the publishers. Therefore, these are multiparty transactions facilitated by smart contracts. The marketplace benefits from Ethereum blockchain's decentralization, security, and programmability features.

The following diagram shows how BAT works:

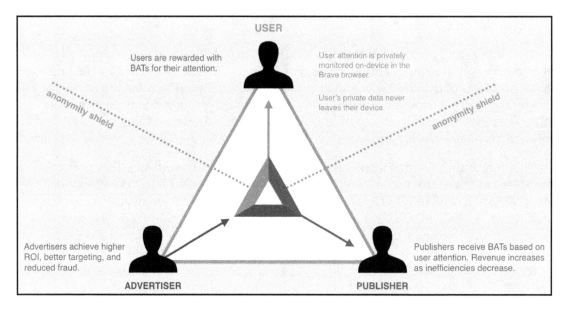

Then, we have applications, which are further away from the realm of financial services, but still benefit from the blockchain architecture and smart contracts. Despite these applications being non-financial, services on their platforms still would have a cost to them that needs to be covered, usually in their native tokens. This category includes applications for supply-chain management, such as tracking components across the industry supply chain, reputation systems, digital IDs, voting, and decentralized governance.

You probably remember WaBi. It's a decentralized application for supply-chain management that aims to solve the problem of counterfeit consumer goods. Product-authenticity verification is done by consumers themselves who scan special RFID labels on the products with their smartphones. **RFID** stands for **radio-frequency identification**. These labels are applied on the products at a designated point of origin along the supply chain and are linked to a unique digital ID for each product. With each scan of the RFID tag, the product ID is checked and verified. For each scan, users are rewarded WaBi tokens, which currently run on the Ethereum blockchain. With the reward transactions, the product ID verification is time- and geo-stamped on the blockchain. WaBi tokens serve as both an incentive mechanism in the form of reward points, and as a currency to purchase products secured by the system. WaBi has been rebranded as Tael. The following diagram shows how WaBi works:

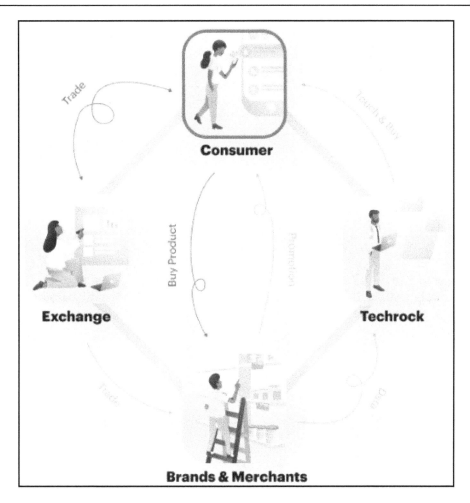

With regards to voting and decentralized governance applications, an interesting example is **Horizon State**. They build voting systems using the Ethereum blockchain. Voting is done with their native decision tokens, which can be used for all sorts of political elections, opinion polls, and shareholder votes. The benefits of security and immutability that blockchain brings to the voting process are all important.

We've made quite a journey through the extensive universe of the decentralized applications of Web 3, and you should have a good idea of what they're all about. Now let's cover another important aspect of the Ethereum platform. Besides an environment for building decentralized applications, Ethereum provides a platform for crowdfunding these projects. Let's see how this works next.

Ethereum and initial coin offerings

Ethereum has made it very easy for anyone to create and issue virtual tokens on its blockchain. This is done with the help of standardized Ethereum smart contracts, such as ERC20. In this way, people, businesses, or governments can issue their own virtual currencies, assets, or application tokens using the Ethereum blockchain, without the need to build their own blockchains.

The facility of issuing new digital tokens or coins based on Ethereum stimulated a massive wave of new start-up ventures that innovate and fund their projects on the Ethereum blockchain. The funding comes in the form of **initial coin offerings** (**ICOs**), also known as token-generation events. In this way, start-ups can issue digital tokens that can be exchanged for services on their future platforms. They can also issue tokens that represent financial instruments, such as equity shares. These two broad classes of tokens are commonly referred to as utility and security tokens. This mechanism turned out to be a huge enabler of crowdfunding on the blockchain. It even exceeded traditional early stage venture capital multiple times, one of the typical ways that start-ups raise funding. This can be seen in the following screenshot:

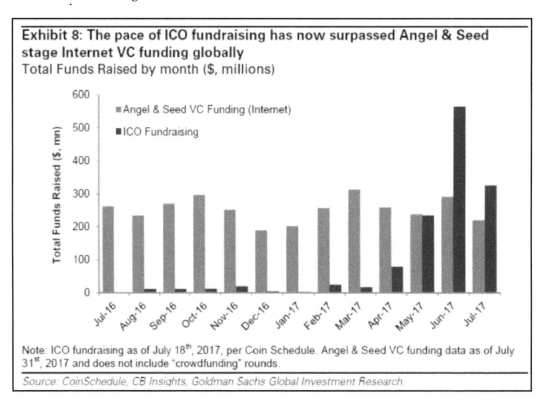

Exhibit 8: The pace of ICO fundraising has now surpassed Angel & Seed stage Internet VC funding globally
Total Funds Raised by month ($, millions)

Note: ICO fundraising as of July 18th, 2017, per Coin Schedule. Angel & Seed VC funding data as of July 31st, 2017 and does not include "crowdfunding" rounds.

Source: CoinSchedule, CB Insights, Goldman Sachs Global Investment Research.

Projects that run ICOs based on an Ethereum token, which is quick and easy to issue, retain flexibility afterward to use the Ethereum blockchain for their future service offering, or to build their own blockchain. This is a business decision that needs to be taken on a case-by-case basis.

Some business applications can benefit from their own dedicated blockchains for industry-specific reasons or due to scalability issues. The Ethereum blockchain currently doesn't have unlimited capacity to handle all applications and their transactions at the scale needed for mass adoption. Ethereum is still an early-stage and experimental technology. Thus, further progress is needed to upgrade it to a point where its network will be robust enough to handle all the traffic of a large, decentralized application's ecosystem.

It should be noted that Ethereum is not the first, nor the only, blockchain platform for decentralized applications and ICOs. For instance, NEO, which many people call the Ethereum of China, is another such platform. Even Bitcoin has a smart contracts functionality that can be used for this, as we saw earlier when we discussed the colored coins and **Counterparty** projects.

Another platform for decentralized applications is **Mastercoin**, later rebranded to Omni. Mastercoin did its own ICO in 2013, raising $5,000,000 worth of Bitcoin to build its protocol layer on top of the Bitcoin blockchain.

One of the most notable examples of a project that did its ICO using the Mastercoin protocol is MadeSafe—a platform for distributed computing resources, such as file storage and processing power. This application is similar, in a way, to popular cloud storage services such as Dropbox, Google Drive, or Amazon Cloud, but it's decentralized on the blockchain, and it rents out the spare disk space of its network nodes rather than a centralized server.

Storj is another distributed data storage project. It initially started building its platform on the Counterparty protocol, thus relying on the Bitcoin blockchain infrastructure. Later on, the Storj team decided to move the application to the Ethereum blockchain and issued a standard Ethereum ERC20 token.

Another project, called **Civic**, is making a move in the opposite direction. Civic is a decentralized application for personal-identity verification. They launched their ICO by issuing a token on Ethereum, but are moving their platform to the Bitcoin blockchain with the help of Rootstock. **Rootstock** (**RSK**) is a new platform for decentralized applications that run on top of the Bitcoin blockchain. It aims to combine Ethereum-type smart contracts with the security of the Bitcoin blockchain, which is second to none.

To illustrate this point further, we can compare decentralized applications to mobile applications. Projects can pick their platform of choice for their decentralized application in the same way they can develop mobile apps for Android or Apple phones. Android and iOS are two separate platforms with their own protocols and app stores. Any mobile application can be built for either platform, and the user interface may look the same, but the application code in each case would be different.

Of course, projects always have the option to build their own blockchains. **Sia** and **Filecoin** are two other distributed data-storage applications that are building their own blockchains rather than using Ethereum or Bitcoin. We'll focus more on application-specific and industry-specific blockchains in the coming chapters.

The important point to make here is that various blockchain platforms for decentralized applications exist. They provide general-purpose technology to develop and launch such applications. Ethereum is currently the premier platform for decentralized apps and ICOs.

Now, you should have a good idea what decentralized applications are. Let's go a step further into the future to discuss an even more ambitious idea envisaged by the Ethereum founders: decentralized autonomous organizations.

Decentralized autonomous organizations

Decentralized autonomous organizations (DAOs) are envisaged as autonomous entities that operate on the blockchain in a completely automated, transparent, and publicly-managed way.

These entities can also be referred to as DACs. The relationships among investors, owners, employees, and other stakeholders, as well as the assets and resources of such enterprises, are managed by smart contracts on the blockchain, rather than by legal contracts and organizational bylaws.

Imagine a set of smart contracts that cooperate to manage an organization according to its mission statement and a set of logical rules. They can autonomously execute a business strategy according to plan. They can buy resources or services, hire people or machines for jobs, pay suppliers, partners, and employees, run marketing activities, logistics, distribution, sales, and so on, in order to create value for their owners. Well, we aren't there yet! But we already have many of the building blocks. So, we can contemplate the design of a future corporation without managers, but just shareholders, money, and software, where shareholders would provide the capital and have direct control over the software that runs the day-to-day operations.

A DAO is currently more of a philosophical concept than a strictly-defined type of business or social entity. It's a vision for the next evolutionary step in organizational theory and design, toward more decentralization and autonomy.

It can be argued that all public blockchains, starting from Bitcoin, in fact, represent DAOs to a certain extent. However, blockchains without a Turing-complete programming language has limited smart contract capabilities. DAOs need smart contracts that can represent complex stakeholder relationships and business logic.

Bitcoin, Ethereum, and other blockchain protocols and systems can be regarded as general-purpose technology that enables the creation and operation of DAOs. In that sense, DAOs can be described as decentralized applications whose governance and operations run on the blockchain.

The important thing here, for all practical purposes, is that DAOs can potentially function with very little, or without any, human involvement in their management. All administrative and business processes can be programmed in smart contracts, at least in theory. Human intervention may be needed only to maintain and upgrade the smart algorithms.

You know that many manufacturing processes have been automated with machines in recent history (such as a robot arm that assembles cars in a high-tech factory). DAOs represent an equivalent automation in organizational management.

To make DAOs even more autonomous, in the future they may include artificial intelligence in the form of machine learning algorithms implemented in smart contracts. Such AI-based smart contracts are referred to as **autonomous agents**. However, implementing this kind of high-tech solution is still pretty much in the realm of science fiction.

If artificial intelligence indeed finds its way into the mix, things can get very, very interesting. For example, machine learning may enable DAOs to maintain and upgrade their own software and hardware without any help from humans. It remains to be seen what the future holds for DAOs. Hopefully, we'll avoid invoking Skynet from the Terminator movies or agent Smith from the Matrix...

The DAO

There is one more thing we should clarify regarding DAOs. In 2016, a project called **The DAO** launched a $150,000,000 ICO, which was the biggest at the time. The funding came in Ethereum's native cryptocurrency: ether. The DAO team collected 11,500,000 ether, which was 15% of all existing ether at that point. The idea was for The DAO to become a decentralized, self-governed, venture capital fund, without any management or board of directors, where token-holders vote directly on investment opportunities and on the future development of the project:

Unfortunately, the code of its smart contract had some serious flaws, which went unnoticed initially by its development team. However, they were noticed by the community and some experts voiced their concerns. Despite the warnings, the project went on, and soon after the launch, it got hacked. Around one third of the ether raised was diverted to an account controlled by hackers. To resolve the situation, the core Ethereum developer team had to make an upgrade in the Ethereum software, known as a hard fork, which caused the split of the network between Ethereum and Ethereum Classic. That's why there are two Ethereum networks currently, each with its own native cryptoassets and ecosystem. They share the same technological fundamentals, at least as of the time of the hard fork. Then one part of the Ethereum community supported the reversal of the DAO hack, while the other part did not, insisting on preserving the immutable nature of the blockchain above all. The majority of the community supported the hard fork, given the importance and consequences of the hack, and thus Ethereum ended up being the main chain.

A minority of hardcore blockchain maximalists insisted on maintaining the DAO hack transaction as it is, in the blockchain, so they backed Ethereum Classic, which is the original Ethereum blockchain with the entire transaction history, but a smaller community, market capitalization, and ecosystem, at present. Since the hard fork, Ethereum and Ethereum Classic have followed separate development paths.

It's important to distinguish between the generic DAO concept and the specific project called The DAO. We're going to see more DAOs in the future. There's no innovation without experimentation, which is a trial-and-error process. The community, and most importantly, the developers of such new projects, should learn their lessons and try to avoid such errors in the future.

Summary

Let's recap everything we've covered about Ethereum.

We started by introducing Vitalik Buterin, the polymath visionary whiz kid, who came up with the idea of Ethereum, at the age of 19, in 2013. We learned that the key differentiating factor of Ethereum is its Turing-completeness. The Ethereum Virtual Machine and Solidity programming language enable a complete set of smart contracts that can be programmed to do pretty much any computer task or function. This powerful innovation unlocked unprecedented opportunities to create an entire universe of decentralized applications that run on the blockchain. But it also created some additional risks of software bugs and hacks, as we have seen with The DAO, Parity wallet, and multiple other mishaps. Hopefully, with time and experience, such cybersecurity threats in the blockchain space will be mitigated and greatly reduced.

We presented an overview of some potential use cases for decentralized applications and examples of some actual projects developing such applications. We also touched upon the even more ambitious and futuristic concept of DAOs.

So far in this book, we've presented the Bitcoin and Ethereum blockchain protocols and various decentralized applications that run on them. In the next chapter, we'll discuss some industry-specific applications that have their own blockchains. Stay tuned as we go deeper and deeper into the world of blockchain technology!

11
Blockchains Focused on Specific Sectors and Use Cases

Welcome back on our blockchain journey! We have covered a lot of ground so far, from the history of money and why blockchain cryptoassets make sense to the foundational technologies of Bitcoin and Ethereum. Now that you have a good understanding of Bitcoin and Ethereum, which pioneered the first and second generation of this technology, we can move on and introduce some other interesting projects related to these technologies.

The following topics will be covered in this chapter:

- The different categories of blockchain
- Sector-specific blockchains
- Private blockchains

The different categories of blockchain

As we mentioned in the previous chapters, we can put blockchains into two broad categories, depending on who owns them and how accessible are they.

First, we have public blockchains, which are open source projects, with free access for anyone to join the network and use it, support it, contribute to it, or build businesses on it.

Then, we have private blockchains, which are not open source, and have restricted access to only users and entities who have been approved by the organization that owns and manages the network.

In each of these categories, there are projects with general purpose blockchains such as Ethereum; however, there are also some application-specific blockchains present. General purpose technology is used to provide foundational infrastructure and building blocks to create applications on top of. For example, you can refer to pretty much any decentralized application based on Ethereum. With that said, it's essentially a one-size-fits-all toolbox.

On the other hand, tailored blockchains or application-specific blockchains are blockchains with industry-specific use cases. They focus just on one sector or market, where they build innovative business models and provide solutions leveraging the strengths of blockchain technology. These blockchains focus on just one sector. That said, they can still be open source for everyone to access.

Sector-specific public blockchains

Let's move on and have a look at a few sector-specific public blockchain projects.

An interesting public blockchain platform in the social media space is **Steem**. It has an innovative business model, which provides incentives to users to contribute high quality content and to participate on the platform. These incentives come in Steem's native cryptoassets, which are traded on exchanges and have real monetary value. There is a simple rationale for this: quality content increases traffic to the platform, thus bringing in more users. The more users a social media platform has, the more valuable it is. This is called a **positive network effect**. Therefore, members contributing high quality content or helping to curate content on the platform get their fair share of the value that's created.

The platform itself is a cross between Reddit and Medium, which are popular for blog posts and social commentary on specific topics. Like Medium, people can write and publish long blog posts, and like Reddit, they can share content and links from anywhere on the internet. Posts are upvoted, downvoted, and commented on by other users. The following diagram shows how Steem works in detail:

DTube takes decentralized social media a step further. It is a video sharing and streaming platform, similar to YouTube, built as an application on the Steem blockchain. The principles it operates on are the same as those of Steem: content contributors are rewarded in Steem's native cryptoassets, but the focus is on video rather than blog posts. The main benefits of a decentralized YouTube are more fair value distribution among content creators and users, no annoying ads, and censorship resistance. The following diagram further explains DTube:

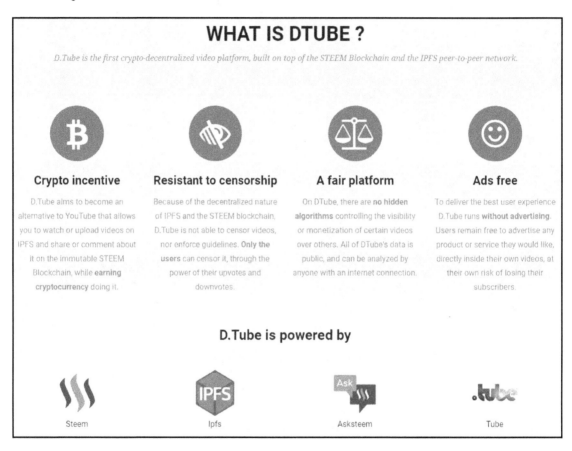

Now, let's take a look at another industrial application: supply-chain management and the **Internet of Things (IoT)**.

Blockchain and IoT

We already mentioned that blockchain has a use case in supply-chain management and we presented a couple of applications for that built on Ethereum, WaBi, and Modum. We can expand this idea to a broader use case: IoT. IoT can be defined as a network of smart devices that are capable of autonomously connecting to the Internet and communicating with each other. The following diagram shows the flow of IoT:

Actually, you should be quite familiar with such devices; in fact, one of them is probably in your pocket, your smartphone. Just like we have mass adoption of smartphones today (and remember that phones were not always smart), the vision of IoT is to have smart meters, smart grids, smart cars, smart homes, and even smart cities. The next generation of IoT devices includes smart electricity meters, which automatically send measurements of electricity usage by a house to the utility company for billing. This is part of the idea for smart homes, smart grids, and smart cities, where all sorts of home appliances and infrastructure can communicate with each other over the Internet and perform tasks autonomously. Other examples include wearable devices, heart monitoring implants, chips for tagging and monitoring animals, smart connected cars, and so on. Pretty much any physical object or device you can think of can be designed with some computational intelligence and Internet connectivity. IoT devices can have various sensors and technologies for collecting, measuring, and transmitting data, like the RFID chips that WaBi uses or the temperature sensors and Bluetooth that Modum uses.

Some other notable projects combining IoT with the secure and immutable record keeping of blockchains and smart contract automation include VeChain and Waltonchain, which are launching their own dedicated blockchains:

All these projects target different industry verticals, such as consumer goods, luxury goods, pharma, auto sector, logistics, shipping, and so on. They also tailor their solutions in slightly different ways, by using different types of sensors, general-purpose blockchains like Ethereum, or their own dedicated blockchains. However, the overall idea and business application are the same; they are all trying to deliver effective and efficient supply-chain management solutions through the convergence of IoT, blockchain, and smart contracts technologies. And this is a valid **unique selling proposition** (USP).

Our landscape of blockchain applications is gradually expanding and the horizon is nowhere to be seen yet. Next, we'll cover the important topic of privacy-focused blockchain technologies.

Private blockchains

In this day and age, privacy is an ever more rare and valuable commodity. Technologies such as the Internet and smartphones have brought unprecedented ease and speed to information discovery. Just like everything, these developments have their pros and cons. On the positive side, useful information, education, and knowledge can be spread quickly and empower people globally. People around the world who have traditionally been disadvantaged from information asymmetries now have the tools that can give them an equal opportunity to pursue their personal development goals and dreams. However, on the downside, the same technology can empower entities with dubious agendas to spy on people, like Big Brother in *Nineteen Eighty-Four*, George Orwell's classic dystopian novel published in 1949.

There are malicious hackers who break into central servers to steal valuable private information and nobody is fully protected against that. It has happened to pretty much all big multinational banks, multibillion dollar corporations handling personal data such as Experian, tech giants, and even top security government agencies such as the **National Security Agency** (**NSA**). When there is a clear valuable target or central point of failure, hackers always find a way.

Moreover, there are numerous data brokers who make business out of people's personal information. They collect it lawfully or not, analyze it, and sell it to anyone who is willing to pay—usually advertisers, but also political campaigns as the recent case with Facebook and Cambridge Analytica showed.

How blockchain affects privacy

Where the boundaries are between personal privacy protection versus intrusion for a higher purpose is a hot topic of public debate right now. This is normal, given the technological advances of our society discussed so far.

Privacy is a desirable feature, not just for criminals, but also by regular people and businesses who don't want their personal and confidential information to be compromised and monetized by third parties. Given the transparency of public blockchains, many businesses may not feel comfortable to use them for conducting their operations. There is a lot of sensitive business information such as transactions with suppliers, quantities, and other private supply-chain details, as well as employee pay, which may not be appropriate to be stored on a transparent, public blockchain. Such information usually is kept as a trade secret, as it can be a source of important competitive advantage, after all.

Therefore, in parallel with the technologies powering the information age, solutions have been in development to secure privacy and mitigate risks of personal data breaches. These solutions mostly revolve around cryptography. You probably remember our cryptography overview from Chapter 5, *Five Forces of Bitcoin – #2 Cryptography*. Here, we'll have a look at several blockchain cryptoassets, which have made advances in their privacy features beyond what Bitcoin offers. They focus, first and foremost, on delivering excellent privacy solutions to the market.

It is a common misconception that Bitcoin is an anonymous currency. Actually, it is pseudo-anonymous, since all transactions can be seen by anyone using a block explorer like those we described earlier. Bitcoin transactions don't show usernames, but they show their public addresses, which can then be linked to the owners. This can be done at any point where users are required to do KYC, or otherwise disclose their identity, in order to transact. Such network nodes can include exchanges, other regulated financial institutions, airlines, e-commerce websites, or other merchants, which may accept payments in Bitcoin.

Blockchain cryptoassets dealing with privacy

Therefore, other solutions are needed to fulfil the market need for private transactions. A level of privacy similar to that of physical cash is very hard to achieve with digital money. But when there is a problem and market demand, solutions are soon to follow. Hence, here come the privacy coins! Monero, ZCash, and DASH are the top privacy-focused blockchain cryptoassets in terms of adoption, capitalization, and advanced technological innovations:

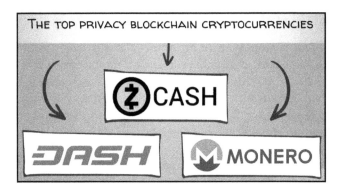

Monero is widely considered the digital currency with the strongest privacy features, thanks to its cryptography using ring signatures. Monero's cryptography is more complex than that of Bitcoin and most other cryptoassets, so we won't get into all the technical details. But to give you an idea, transactions in Bitcoin are digitally signed with personal cryptographic keys, so that anyone can see the addresses of the sender and the receiver, as well as the transaction amounts. This proves that the sender owns the money being transferred. It is similar in its purpose and effect to signing a check from your bank.

On the other hand, Monero's ring signatures are described as follows:

> *"Digital signatures that specify a group of possible signers, such that the verifier can't tell which member actually produced the signature."*

Therefore, transactions in Monero appear to be signed by a large pool of users rather than a specific user. The ring signature only proves that the transaction was sent by someone in that pool, but it doesn't disclose exactly who. The Monero protocol allows for complete user privacy in terms of amounts, origins, and destinations for transactions, and it has a mechanism to prevent double-spending. In these features, it is similar to ZCash with its zero-knowledge proofs or zk-SNARKs, which we'll discuss next.

Launched in 2016, ZCash brought a new privacy technology to the blockchain market called zero-knowledge proofs with its zk-SNARKs protocol. ZCash provides optionality for users to either send regular transactions, like in Bitcoin, or to send private transactions where no information is revealed, other than that the transactions are valid. The project is led by Zooko Wilcox, who was previously part of David Chaums's DigiCash in the 1990s.

DASH is another blockchain cryptoasset supporting private transactions. For this purpose, it uses a different protocol, which basically mixes many transactions together, to form kind of a large multiparty pooled transaction. In this way, it scrambles the different components of each transaction and makes it nearly impossible for an external observer to put the pieces together and figure out who sent what to whom.

Summary

You now get the idea of privacy and its important implications in business and everyday life. In this chapter, we learned about public blockchains and how they affect our daily life. We also learned how blockchain can be used with IoT to enhance various sectors. Also, we learned how blockchain affects privacy and helps in securing transactions. Finally, we learned about some cryptoassets and how they deal with security.

In the next chapter, we will learn about corporate blockchains! Stay tuned!

12
Corporate Blockchains

In the previous chapter, we learned about different types of blockchains, such as sector-specific blockchains and private blockchains. Now it's time to describe another important, but largely unfamiliar to most people, part of the blockchain universe: private permissioned blockchains, or in other words, corporate blockchains. In this chapter, we will cover the following topics:

- Introduction to corporate blockchains
- R3 Corda
- Hyperledger
- Enterprise Ethereum Alliance
- Private blockchains for business

Introduction to corporate blockchains

Corporate blockchains are different from public blockchains such as Bitcoin, Ethereum, and the other projects discussed so far, mainly in one key aspect: access to the network. While in public blockchains, anyone can download some open source software, join the network, and use it, in private blockchains, access to the network is restricted. Corporations, government entities, or other organizations can build their own private blockchains to serve their business or administrative purposes. Such private blockchains are typically more centralized and much closer to a distributed database or ledger in their architecture and functions. This is because they don't need a decentralized trust model like Bitcoin and other public blockchains.

If all blockchain participants are known, and have been pre-approved and vetted, there isn't much need to have complex consensus algorithms based on game theory. Network nodes can easily agree on the latest version of the blockchain database, as they all know and trust each other by virtue of being part of the same organization.

As we mentioned in `Chapter 11`, *Blockchains Focused on Specific Sectors and Use Cases*, public blockchains may not be suitable for everything and everyone. For many internal business processes, private blockchains may be a better option.

Nowadays, the value of blockchain technology for business, government, and personal use is widely accepted around the world. Most large international banks and other financial institutions have been developing their internal blockchain projects for a few years now. Established technology companies, such as IBM, have also joined the bandwagon. The same goes for shipping industry leaders, such as Maersk, that are interested in how blockchain can optimize their supply-chain management. These large corporations have found that the best way to develop their blockchain projects is to cooperate in industrial alliances, consortiums, or partnerships with each other. This may involve industry incubators where start-up teams collaborate with corporations to develop solutions for industrial use. Next, we'll have a look at some of the most prominent cross-industry consortiums for blockchain development.

R3 Corda

R3 started as an alliance of nine banks in 2015, with the aim of developing blockchain infrastructure for the financial sector. It has grown to include over 200 financial institutions in 2018. Banks believe that blockchain technology could save them money by making their operations faster, more efficient, and more transparent. They are racing to build products using the technology that will generate new revenue, with dozens of patent applications filed for blockchain-based products by banks around the world.

R3's main project is Corda, a blockchain, or as they call it, a **distributed ledger technology (DLT)** platform, designed specifically for financial agreements between regulated financial institutions. The main difference between Corda and the public blockchains we are already familiar with, such as Bitcoin and Ethereum, is that Corda is based on consensus only between the parties to individual deals, rather than consensus of the entire network. Corda transactions are validated by parties to the transaction rather than a broader pool of unrelated validators. Therefore, the entire transaction database in Corda isn't copied to all network participants. This design also doesn't need a native cryptoasset to incentivize and reward miners to validate transactions, as the PoW consensus algorithm is unnecessary for private deployments. Corda's architecture directly enables regulatory and supervisory observer nodes. Distributed applications can be built on Corda using the **Java Virtual Machine (JVM)**, which facilitates user adoption and interoperability with legacy systems.

Notwithstanding the different design of Corda, the **Chief Technology Officer** (or **CTO**) of R3, Richard G Brown, describes neatly the evolutionary steps that led to Corda's creation, starting with Bitcoin, and giving credit to the brilliant innovation it brought to the world:

> *"Bitcoin's architecture, as I have often written, is a marvel. Its interlocking components are one of those rare examples of something so elegant that they seem obvious in hindsight, yet which required a rare genius to create. Blockchain was the tool that was invented to solve a real problem. We concluded that a blockchain such as the ones underlying Bitcoin or Ethereum or any of the private variations actually provide at least five interlocking, but distinct, services: **Consensus, Validity, Uniqueness, Immutability**, and **Authentication**."*

The core services provided by blockchains

The following shows the various services provided by blockchains and what those services are used for:

- **Consensus**: This is the first, and most important, feature of blockchains and the thing that's probably genuinely new in terms of scale and scope. It allows us to create a world where parties to a shared fact know that the fact they see is the same as the fact that other stakeholders see. Sure, consensus systems and replicated state machines have existed for years, but consensus systems at internet-scale, between untrusting actors, that work in the face of powerful adversaries? That's a step forward! In Bitcoin, the shared facts are things such as: Where are all the Bitcoin (output) that have not yet been spent and what needs to happen for them to be validly spent? The facts are shared between all full-node users. In Ethereum, the shared fact is the state of an abstract virtual computer.

- **Validity**: This feature is about the rules of the game, it defines a clear set of rules for validating transaction.
- **Uniqueness**: This feature refers to the fact that besides following the set of rules for valid transactions, such transactions also need to be unique. In other words, spending the same money twice at the same time can't be allowed. This is the double-spending problem that Bitcoin first solved in a decentralized way.

- **Immutability**: This feature is enforced by the system, not by virtue of past transactions being immutable, but by the fact that the other network participants won't accept a blockchain with past transaction history different from the one they personally store.
- **Authentication**: This feature refers to the design feature of all transactions being authenticated with private keys controlled by users. This eliminates the need for a central authority or system administrator, which can represent a central point of failure.

The conclusion of R3's CTO was that the thing that is genuinely new is the emergence of platforms, shared across the internet between mutually distrusting actors, that allow them to reach consensus about the existence and evolution of facts shared between them.

So, if that's what this is all about, then what are the shared facts that matter in finance? What business problem would we need to have for any of this work to be of any use at all?

And this is the lightbulb moment and the fundamental insight driving the entire Corda project!

The important shared facts between financial institutions are financial agreements, such as the following:

- Bank A and Bank B agree that Bank A owes $1,000,000 USD to Bank B, repayable on demand. This is a cash-demand deposit.
- Bank A and Bank B agree that they are parties to a credit default swap with certain characteristics. This is a derivative contract.
- Bank A and Bank B agree that Bank A is obliged to deliver 1,000 units of Common Stock to Bank B in 3 days' time in exchange for a cash payment of $150,000 USD. This is a delivery-versus-payment agreement.

The financial industry is pretty much defined by the agreements that exist between its firms and these firms share a common problem: the agreement is typically recorded by both parties, in different systems, and very large costs are caused by the need to fix things when these different systems end up believing different things. Multiple research firms have postulated that tens of billions of dollars are spent each year on this problem.

In particular, these systems typically communicate by exchanging messages such as, "I send an update to you and hope that you reach the same conclusion about the new state of the agreement as I do."

Financial institutions spend a lot of money on reconciling their books to check whether all parties are indeed on the same page; and if not, they have to spend even more money to fix any inconsistencies or other issues they uncover.

In order to solve this problem, the Corda system was born. In the words of the CTO, imagine we had a system for recording and managing financial agreements that was shared across firms, that recorded the agreement consistently, and identically, that was visible to the appropriate regulators, and that was built on industry-standard tools, with a focus on interoperability and incremental deployment, and didn't leak confidential information to third parties. A system where one firm could look at its set of agreements with a counterpart and know for sure that, "What I see is what you see and we both know that we see the same thing and we both know that this is what has been reported to the regulator." That's Corda:

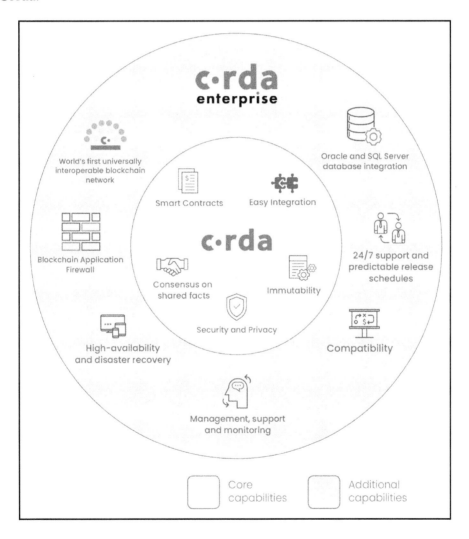

There have been plans to contribute Corda into the Hyperledger project, of which R3 is a member. Hyperledger is another enterprise blockchain-development consortium, which is even broader in scale and scope, with many participants from different industries. We'll look into it next.

Hyperledger

The Hyperledger project is a cross-industry blockchain collaboration launched by the Linux Foundation in December 2015. It focuses on blockchain industrial solutions for finance, banking, IoT, supply chains, healthcare, manufacturing, technology, and other sectors. Currently, it has over 190 member organizations, including industry leaders such as IBM, Intel, American Express, Daimler, Airbus, Fujitsu, Hitachi, Cisco, Accenture, JPMorgan, SAP, NEC, and Baidu.

Hyperledger is an umbrella project, which incubates separate blockchain projects focused on distinct industrial use cases and solutions. Hyperledger projects are built from the ground up to address specific business models and their issues. They are intended as a plug-and-play solution to boost the consortium members' business performance. For that purpose, the fundamental principle to all Hyperledger projects is a **modular approach**. All components of the Hyperledger ecosystem are designed to be interoperable and interchangeable, meaning that they can connect with any other component within that framework. They also must be able to connect with legacy corporate IT systems for enterprise resource planning and so on. Ideally, they would be also able to connect with open public blockchain networks such as Bitcoin and Ethereum.

In their own words, Hyperledger is incubating and promoting enterprise-grade, open source business blockchain technologies, including distributed ledgers, smart contract engines, client libraries, graphical interfaces, utility libraries, and sample applications. Hyperledger provides the underlying open source software, on top of which anyone can set up apps to meet business needs.

So, Hyperledger aims to provide a blockchain platform for distributed applications, kind of like Bitcoin and Ethereum do. But make no mistake, despite being an open source collaboration, Hyperledger targets industrial applications, meant to be deployed mostly as **private permissioned blockchains**. As they themselves say, the optimal focus of Hyperledger is to advance industry goals of distributed ledgers and smart contracts. The overarching Hyperledger design philosophy for permissioned blockchain networks follows a modular approach that enables extensibility and flexibility.

The modular approach they are talking about looks similar to the following image:

Hyperledger Technical Scope

Out of Scope	Custom Applications	App Layer
	API libraries and GUIs Specialized consensus algos Membership policies Gateway Operations dashboard	Value Added Systems
In Scope	Core APIs	Core APIs
	Code execution environment Ledger data structures Modular consensus framework Modular identity services Network peers	Shared Ledger

The reference architecture of Hyperledger identifies several key layers or components: consensus, smart contracts, communication protocol, data storage, cryptography, ID management, governance, APIs, and interconnectivity. This is a major difference from the design of existing public blockchains, such as Bitcoin and Ethereum, where everything is packed into the same blockchain protocol. Therefore, you can imagine that Hyperledger provides more flexibility.

This means that enterprises can choose the consensus algorithm, the smart contract programming language, level of encryption, and so on, that best fit their business needs.

As one of the Hyperledger whitepapers puts it:

> *"Business blockchain requirements vary. Some uses require rapid network consensus systems and short block confirmation times before being added to the chain. For others, a slower processing time may be acceptable in exchange for lower levels of required trust. Scalability, confidentiality, compliance, workflow complexity, and even security requirements differ drastically across industries and uses. Each of these requirements, and many others, represent a potentially unique optimization point for the technology."*

The main benefit of the modular approach is flexibility. With this fundamental principle in mind, Hyperledger develops a range of technological solutions for business applications, including distributed ledgers, smart contracts, code libraries, and graphical user interfaces. It also provides entire sample applications. These common buildings blocks can be reused in many different projects. Any component can be modified independently without affecting the rest of the system. Hyperledger components can be mixed and matched to create tailor-made, enterprise, value-added systems. This framework creates a perfect environment for innovation in the corporate blockchain space.

Let's have a look at it in a bit more detail.

The Hyperledger frameworks

At present, there are 10 Hyperledger projects in incubation, comprising 5 frameworks and 5 tools, as seen in the following screenshot:

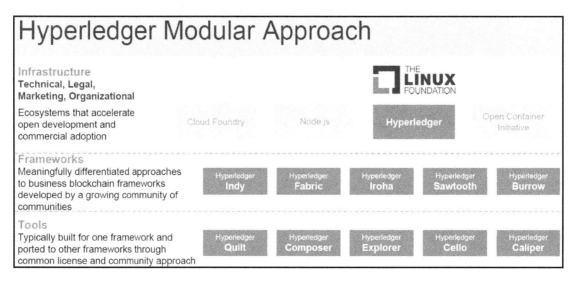

Frameworks represent different approaches to building enterprise blockchains. Here is a brief overview of the main ones.

Hyperledger Fabric

Originally proposed by IBM, Hyperledger Fabric aims to provide a modular, scalable, and secure foundation for industrial blockchain applications. Fabric is a base layer core infrastructure for Hyperledger projects. It exemplifies the modular architecture we described earlier, in order to allow components, such as consensus and smart contracts, to be plug-and-play.

 The Fabric framework is further explained in the following video: `https:/ /www.youtube.com/watch?v=js3Zjxbo8TM`.

Hyperledger Sawtooth

Sawtooth, a project initiated by Intel, delivers another modular platform for distributed enterprise applications. It includes a novel consensus algorithm called **Proof of Elapsed Time** (**PoET**), which is optimized for efficient simulation of the Bitcoin **Proof-of-Work** (**PoW**) consensus in a trusted corporate environment.

The Sawtooth whitepaper goes along familiar lines:

> *"Today's business processes for information sharing are burdened with intermediaries, inefficiencies, and security concerns. Through the use of distributed ledger technology (or blockchains), business processes between companies can be streamlined, and records can be kept in sync without the need for a central authority or manual reconciliation processes. This can help enterprises to reduce their costs and enable them to create entirely new ways of doing business. Sawtooth is a framework for building distributed ledgers for enterprise use, with a focus on modularity and extensibility. Sawtooth builds upon decades of state machine replication research and is designed to support any consensus mechanism or smart contract language."*

The authors also give credit to Bitcoin and Ethereum as inspiration for Hyperledger Sawtooth.

The evolutionary process of deriving new enterprise blockchain solutions from the leading public blockchains is described neatly as follows:

Since the release of Ethereum, a variety of other distributed ledgers implementations have been created to meet the needs of the enterprise. These distributed ledger implementations include software that expands upon existing protocols (such as Bitcoin and Ethereum) and creates entirely new implementations (Corda and Fabric).

Hyperledger Sawtooth borrows many design elements from its public-blockchain predecessors, such as data structures, a peer-to-peer network protocol, and cryptography, and plugs them into the modular Hyperledger framework.

Sawtooth architecture

The Sawtooth architecture has five core components:

- **Peer-to-peer network**: The network used for passing messages and transactions between nodes
- **Distributed log**: A log that contains an ordered list of transactions
- **State machine/smart contract logic** layer for processing the content of those transactions

- **Distributed state**: Storage for storing the resulting state after processing transactions
- **Consensus algorithm**: The algorithm used to achieve consensus across the network on the ordering of transactions and the resulting state

These five core components resemble the five forces that power Bitcoin, which we examined in previous chapters:

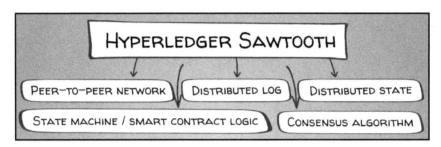

Sawtooth has a permissioned network in order to control who can connect, send transactions, and participate in the consensus.

Also, some default smart contract templates are provided. They're divided by function and grouped into transaction families. This is an innovative idea. There are smart contract templates for managing network settings, and off-the-shelf marketplace and supply chain solutions. There is also a tool for integrating Ethereum smart contracts with Sawtooth.

Users can develop further their own smart contracts and transaction families.

This approach is a little bit different from what we find in general-purpose smart contract platforms. In Ethereum, for example, the same generic instruction set, also known as opcodes, is used for all types of applications. So, smart contracts for financial services, media, supply chain, healthcare, and so on, would use the same toolbox of programming commands.

In Hyperledger Sawtooth, each transaction family has its own smart contract logic, composed of operations specific to that domain. This makes Sawtooth programming both restrictive and secure at the same time, as seen in the following diagram:

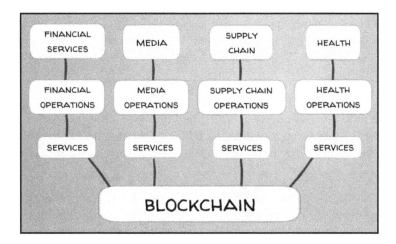

With a smaller code base, the flexibility of what you can do is restricted, but the probability of costly errors is smaller. This design choice follows a similar logic to the reason why the programming capabilities in Bitcoin were restricted from the outset.

Furthermore, Sawtooth enables developers to write smart contracts in a variety of languages, such as Python, JavaScript, C++, Rust, and Go. It's also flexible regarding virtual machines and both the Ethereum and JVMs can be used.

Sawtooth doesn't take a fundamental position on which consensus mechanism is best. Rather, it offers an interface that allows for a variety of consensus protocols to be used.

We can broadly distinguish two main approaches to consensus protocols:

- Lottery consensus
- Voting consensus

The first, also known as **Nakamoto consensus**, elects a leader through some form of lottery. The leader then proposes a new block to be added to the blockchain. In Bitcoin, for example, the first miner to solve the PoW cryptographic puzzle wins the leader-election lottery.

The second approach, also known as **Byzantine Fault-Tolerance** uses votes among consensus participants to elect a leader.

The novel consensus algorithm Sawtooth proposes and adds to its stack is PoET. It is a Nakamoto-style consensus algorithm, designed for trusted enterprise environment. It allows a leader node to be elected randomly based on the time that the node has waited before proposing a block.

PoET provides a similar distribution of results to other lottery algorithms, such as PoW in Bitcoin. The probability of election is proportional to the resources contributed (in this case, resources are general-purpose processors, or CPUs, with a **trusted execution environment**). Code and data loaded inside the trusted execution environment are protected with respect to confidentiality and integrity.

In summary, the key innovations introduced by Sawtooth are the domain-specific smart contract layer and the PoET consensus algorithm. They are essentially modifications of the **Ethereum Virtual Machine** (**EVM**), and the Bitcoin PoW consensus protocol.

The project is neatly summarized by The Sawtooth team, as follows:

Sawtooth is a blockchain platform designed for enterprise usage. Sawtooth builds upon the learnings of platforms before it such as Bitcoin and Ethereum and is designed with a focus on modularity and extensibility. Sawtooth is unique from existing blockchain platforms in that it allows developers to program their smart contracts in a variety of traditional programming languages. Future Sawtooth developments will focus on increasing the throughput and privacy of transactions.

Now, let's move on to the other notable Hyperledger projects.

Hyperledger Iroha

Hyperledger Iroha builds a library of reusable components with a focus on mobile development. These components include libraries for digital signatures, hashing algorithms, transaction protocols, peer-to-peer communication protocols, APIs, Apple, Android, and JavaScript development tools.

Hyperledger Burrow

Hyperledger Burrow is a permissioned smart contract platform, which can integrate with the EVM, in order to run Ethereum smart contracts and distributed applications. It provides interoperability between Hyperledger and Ethereum.

Hyperledger Indy

Hyperledger Indy is an identity-management system. It develops tools, libraries, and reusable components for providing digital identities rooted in blockchains that can be used across different administrative domains and applications.

We'll present some examples of Hyperledger implementations in various industries in the coming section. Next, we'll have a look at another notable project: the Enterprise Ethereum Alliance.

Enterprise Ethereum Alliance

In March 2017, various blockchain startups, research groups, and Fortune 500 companies announced the creation of the **Enterprise Ethereum Alliance** (**EEA**) with 30 founding members. It aims to customize Ethereum for industry players, and thus boost industrial enterprise blockchain solutions using the open source public Ethereum technology.

In 2018, the alliance has grown to over 200 members, making it the largest open source blockchain initiative in the world. Prominent members include established industry leaders across many sectors of the global economy, such as Microsoft, Intel, Samsung, Cisco, Hewlett Packard, Mastercard, JPMorgan, UBS, Credit Suisse, Banco Santander, BNY Mellon, British Petroleum, Shell, Pfizer, Merck, Deloitte, Accenture, Thomson Reuters, and Toyota, as well as emerging leaders in the new blockchain industry, such as ConsenSys and Oraclize.

The companies working on the Enterprise Ethereum Alliance want to create a private permissioned version of Ethereum that can be rolled out for specific purposes and be open only to certified participants. The purpose of the alliance is to create a standard, open source version of Ethereum that can provide a foundation for any specific industrial use case. For instance, banks could create one blockchain platform for themselves, and shipping companies could create another for their own purposes.

The partners will help each other develop the foundations for different use cases, such as post-trade settlement, payments between banks, and supply-chain tracking, while competing on applications and services built atop the networks:

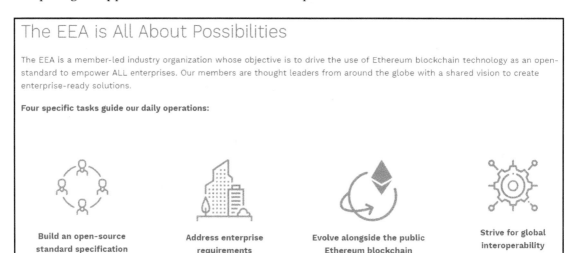

The EEA is All About Possibilities

The EEA is a member-led industry organization whose objective is to drive the use of Ethereum blockchain technology as an open-standard to empower ALL enterprises. Our members are thought leaders from around the globe with a shared vision to create enterprise-ready solutions.

Four specific tasks guide our daily operations:

Build an open-source standard specification

Address enterprise requirements

Evolve alongside the public Ethereum blockchain

Strive for global interoperability

These private systems aren't likely to require an Ether virtual currency, although the companies are hoping to create modules that will allow users to put in and take out individual elements of Ethereum as they choose.

Many companies have already been working to create their own versions of Ethereum for specific purposes. JPMorgan, for instance, has created a version of Ethereum known as Quorum that the bank has been using in tests to move money between JPMorgan branches in different countries. Quorum will become part of the new private version of Ethereum being developed by the alliance.

The choice of Ethereum as a foundational technology by the members of the alliance confirms the level of credibility it has reached in the world. As the principal blockchain architect at Microsoft put it:

In every industry that we come across, Ethereum is usually the first platform that people go to. Ethereum has this massive advantage of having the public network that has been tested for several years.

In its mission statement, the alliance focuses on several key points of development. These points revolve around the maturity, security, and governance of this new technology, as well as business continuity of established corporate infrastructure. Some modifications need to be made to Ethereum's public blockchain to make it suitable for use in enterprises.

Firstly, **integration** with existing business processes and IT infrastructure is necessary. This is important because any corporate initiative to build a smart contract platform will have to import rules and transaction history data from existing databases. Most business information currently resides in the existing private databases of large and small companies. This would need to be integrated with the new emerging blockchain technology for the sake of business continuity and sustainability. For example, a bank would need to transfer associated its rules and history of loan recipients before it starts recording transactions and deploying smart contracts on the Ethereum blockchain.

While the Ethereum alliance focuses on the development of private blockchains, the importance of interoperability with the public Ethereum blockchain is also considered. Their vision is for Ethereum's public and private networks to function like the internet and corporate intranets. They will share standard protocols, such as for data storage and transmission, but will have different configurations for privacy and security, depending on each organization's needs.

As a representative from BNY Mellon put it, even if you create private networks, if you can anchor them to public networks, you get an extremely strong set of links together.

Governance and compliance with existing and emerging regulatory frameworks is also a challenge that needs to be addressed by the blockchain community. This is especially important for highly-regulated industries, such as finance. The Enterprise Ethereum Alliance aims to become a governance and standards-setting body for Ethereum enterprise applications. Customizing smart contracts to work in established organizations requires permissions and access levels from different entities. The alliance will design a framework for industry-wide governance and implementation of smart contracts with input from its members.

Continued and accelerated **innovation** of the Ethereum technology for business is also a major focus point for the alliance. It aims to retain compatibility with and enhance the public Ethereum network. If Ethereum's smart contracts are to reach their promised business potential and change the way we conduct transactions, its public blockchain must include contributions from a diverse set of stakeholders. Familiar frameworks and the standardization of technical requisites will clear roadblocks for developers interested in innovating within the Ethereum ecosystem. The alliance aims to plug in new features based on use cases developed in-house and contribute to Ethereum's roadmap.

In summary, the EEA aims to facilitate and accelerate enterprise adoption of Ethereum-based blockchain technology. The top priorities for the alliance now include ensuring scalability and security.

Private blockchains for business

This will conclude our overview of industrial private blockchain projects. To recap, in the previous sections, we presented three leading initiatives for developing and promoting enterprise-grade blockchain technology for industrial use: R3, Hyperledger, and EEA. Each has its own community of members, developers, and other contributors, and they all have their own version of foundational blockchain technology serving as a basis for further ecosystem development, as shown in the following diagram:

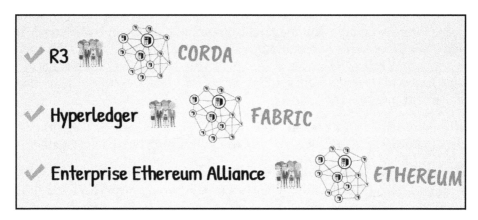

The premise, upon which Hyperledger Fabric, R3 Corda, and other private permissioned blockchain projects build upon, is that enterprise-grade blockchain solutions will operate in a trusted environment. This is due to the nature of how businesses tend to operate in the real world with known and endorsed partners. This premise has implications on the architecture of private permissioned blockchains, which is different from that of public permission-less blockchains such as Bitcoin and Ethereum. The game theory settings in these two scenarios are different.

Public blockchains, open to everyone, need a complex consensus mechanism with a native cryptoasset, such as PoW, to enforce the security of the network – in other words, to ensure that all participants are incentivized to play by the rules.

Private blockchains, where all participants are pre-approved, don't need the same type of consensus mechanism, nor cryptocurrency. Instead, other factors, such as trusted business relationships, build trust in the system, which is a more traditional approach.

So, having examined both public and private blockchains, we can conclude that there's a significant conceptual difference between them and it's mainly in the approach to how they build trust in the system, as seen in the following diagram:

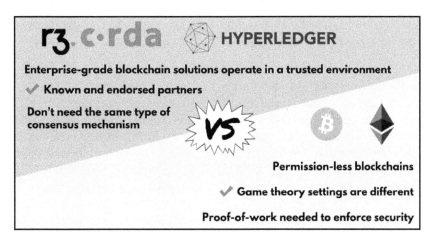

Public blockchains have introduced a real breakthrough solution to an existential global problem – how to transfer value among unknown parties, without a need for the parties to trust each other, and without the presence of a central authority. In contrast, private blockchains take some of the innovations of public blockchains, such as decentralized peer-to-peer transaction settlement and smart contacts, and bring these to a familiar corporate environment of trusted business partners.

It can be argued that the pioneering public blockchains introduced brilliant and disruptive technological solutions, which have their own challenges to achieve mass adoption, in terms of scalability, interoperability, privacy, and governance. They are, however, the most decentralized economic systems the world has ever known.

Private blockchain projects introduce their own solutions to the issues of scalability, interoperability, privacy, and governance, which their public peers have, but this is at the cost of less decentralization. They bring some of the benefits of public blockchains to the traditional setting of corporate walled gardens and restricted-access networks. But this creates single points of failure. What if a system administrator that's in charge of granting access to the corporate network gets hacked or otherwise corrupted? How many large corporations and government organizations have had their internal IT systems compromised in the past? The list is very, very long.

In this sense, we can compare public blockchains to the internet, and private blockchains to corporate intranets. While private blockchain technology will most likely bring great efficiencies and cost savings to the established players in finance and industry, with things such as optimizing their internal processes and supply chains, this would still have a mild effect in comparison to how public blockchains might be able to change the world. These two paths represent the difference between a gradual evolution and a disruptive revolution.

So, what does the future hold? As always, the reality is probably in the middle. Private blockchains have their own merits in the current business environment and are being designed for user-friendly adoption by organizations in their present shape and form, without too much costly and unnecessary corporate restructuring. On the other hand, public blockchains have the potential to completely change the way business, as we know it, is done, and redesign the economic landscape. To reach that point, however, they will need to address some pressing issues limiting their development and mass user adoption. These are the issues we already mentioned, but it's worth repeating them because they are so critical: **scalability**, **interoperability**, **privacy**, and **governance**. There are a number of projects, currently in development, that are trying to resolve these issues. They are being advanced by the development teams of leading established public blockchains, such as Bitcoin and Ethereum, as well as by a bunch of new ambitious projects aiming to lead the next generation of blockchain technology.

The race is open, and competition is heated. Who will succeed first? Do private permissioned blockchains hold the keys to corporate success? Will open public blockchains completely change the way we do business and reshape the concept of a business enterprise as we know it? If so, which public blockchains will be the winners? Will Bitcoin and Ethereum preserve their leadership or will they get replaced by a new competitor? Is it going to be a winner-takes-all game, or are we going to have a more decentralized landscape in line with the fundamental principle of this new technology? After all, we already have huge tech monopolies with unbelievable market power, such as Google, Amazon, and Facebook. Why does the world need to invent a great new decentralized way of doing things, just to replace the old corporate behemoths with new ones? How will the future business landscape look?

Perhaps we'll have hybrid implementations of public and private blockchains. Some projects have already envisioned this solution and are trying to build it in their business models. Maybe we can take a look at the auto industry for a useful example – electric vehicles are widely proclaimed as the future, but currently we have a market with traditional cars running on gas, electric cars, and hybrids. This shows that innovation that completely replaces pre-existing solutions doesn't happen overnight.

Summary

The Ethereum technology is still in its nascent stage and will have to overcome several roadblocks – technical and regulatory – before it becomes fully-functional and eligible for mass business adoption. In this chapter, we learned that initiatives, such as the EEA, are important forums for established industry leaders and disruptive start-ups must work and innovate together toward changing the world for the better. We learned about various corporate blockchains and how they affect daily business.

Well, as the old saying goes: time will tell. Let's now take a look at some practical examples of how blockchain business adoption is progressing. Then we'll discuss the present issues the technology is facing, and how are they being addressed, so that public blockchains can get to the next level and solve the scalability, interoperability, privacy, and governance conundrum. We'll cover these important topics in the following chapters. Stay tuned!

13
The Disruptive Potential of Blockchain Technology

The world has seen several innovations that have radically transformed the way economic value is created and captured by individuals and companies. Inventions like the wheel, the compass, intercontinental travel, the steam engine, railways, the automobile, the airplane, the computer, and the internet have played a major role in shaping the global economy.

In this chapter, we want to give you an idea of how profound the impact of blockchain will be, a decade or two from now. We will cover the following topics in this chapter:

- Blockchain and financial services
- Trade finance on the blockchain
- Blockchain and insurance
- Investment banking and blockchain
- Blockchain and financial regulation
- Blockchain and the retail sector
- Blockchain and intellectual property
- Blockchain and the food sector
- Blockchain and the transportation sector
- Blockchain and the global tech giants

Blockchain and financial services

Thirty years ago, the internet came on the stage, and it took less than a decade to scale it to mass adoption as a general-purpose technology. People quickly embraced it as another instrument shortening the distance between them and allowing them to communicate in real time.

Now, for the first time in history, a person located in the US can send an email to someone in Japan, and the message will be received instantly without the need to use the services of a courier or post stamps. It is as simple as clicking a button and the message arrives in the recipient's inbox.

Then of course, a lot of other amazing use cases have followed the birth of the internet.

People started creating informational websites, watching videos online, going on the internet for location services, communication with friends and colleagues, exchanging files, ordering food and shopping online, along with countless other applications that are emerging even to this very day.

How many industries have been completely reshaped in the process? Let's find out now.

Traditional libraries and encyclopedias aren't the go-to source for information anymore. Everybody uses Google, Wikipedia, Reddit, Quora, and other online services to find answers to their questions.

When we say map, we don't think of actual paper maps, but refer to Google Maps—the popular GPS location service seen in the following diagram:

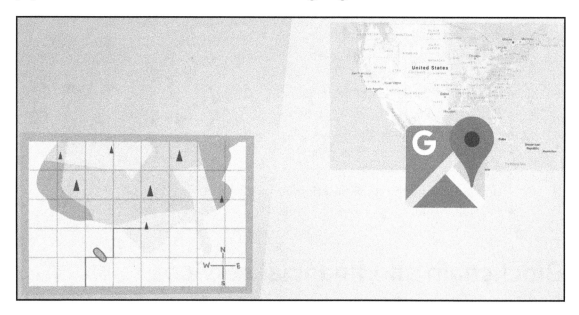

Blockbuster, the world's largest video rental company, went bankrupt because it failed to adapt to a changing environment where online streaming and digital distribution became the prevalent form of business. On the other hand, Netflix managed to build a superb business model that was well positioned for the opportunities offered by a digital world.

People do not buy music tapes anymore, but they subscribe for services such as Spotify and Pandora, which, similar to Netflix, managed to come up with the winning formula.

The examples of industries that have been completely reshaped by the internet are countless. And the companies that managed to win big are the ones that embraced the new technology and built their business models around it.

How blockchain comes into the picture

This is a truly fascinating time to keep up with technological innovation. We have created this book with the hope that it will inspire you and will foster your interest in blockchain technology, and not just the speculative aspect of it with the thousands of new cryptoassets coming out. If you want to be truly empowered by it, you should try to understand what it actually does and how it can be applied in the real world.

Think of this moment as the mid 1990s when the internet was emerging, but very few people had an idea how it functioned and what applications it might have.

Well, we already presented you the fundamentals of blockchain and why it is such an exciting new technology. Now, it is time to consider how it can be applied and integrated into our world.

We are not going to talk about cryptocurrencies and market speculation. Hopefully, we didn't just lose half of our audience with this statement!

Instead, we will talk about ideas and technology applications. This is something much more valuable in the long run.

So, now we are going to examine the potential impact blockchain might have on several industries in the future, and what business opportunities can arise when this comes to fruition.

It isn't a coincidence that we are starting with the financial sector. As we already said, the financial services industry has been stagnant for quite some time and the technology known as the internet of money has the potential to disrupt the existing status quo.

This isn't a question of if, but more of a question of how and when.

Why banks shouldn't ignore blockchain

Given that we want to describe how banking services could be disrupted in the future, it will be best to start by distinguishing between the two main types of banking, commercial and investment banking.

Commercial banks are the regular banks we see around us, providing loans to the population and storing its savings. These are the so-called traditional banks that are mainly involved with deposit taking and credit giving activities. These banks collect deposits from people and companies who have savings and then lend the money to borrowers. The difference between the interest they pay to depositors and the interest they charge borrowers is called **spread** and represents commercial banks' main source of revenue. In addition, over the years, commercial banks started offering some other services, such as international money transfers, custody, letters of credit, forex dealing, and escrow accounts:

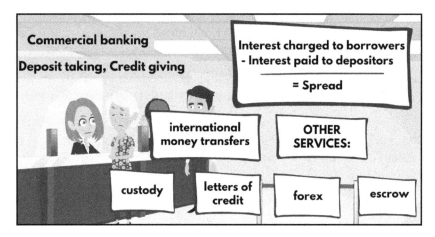

Investment banks, on the other hand, deal with more sophisticated operations. They assist businesses in major corporate events such as when they are about to make an initial public offering and list their shares on a stock exchange, or when they are involved in mergers and acquisitions.

Since these two business models are quite different, it makes sense to analyze them separately.

Let's focus on commercial banks, since they impact the everyday lives of most people.

The commercial banking business model would need to be updated in a major way with the advent of blockchain technology.

In his 2015 letter to shareholders, Jamie Dimon (the CEO and Chairman of JP Morgan Chase, one of the largest banks in the world) said that there are hundreds of startups with lots of brains and money who are hard at work on alternatives to traditional banking.

After the boom of 2017, and the huge amounts of capital, research, and development pouring into blockchain technology, it wouldn't be an exaggeration to say that Silicon Valley and tech startups are not simply coming. They are advancing at full speed to disrupt the world and banking is the first sector to be impacted.

But why should banks even bother?

Their business model has been valid for hundreds of years and the internet hasn't created any significant disruptions so far.

Well, this time we are talking about the internet of money, and here things are different.

Traditional banks' core business revolves around deposit taking and credit giving. If people stop depositing their funds and bank deposits decrease, commercial banks would not be able to finance the loans they give to borrowers at a cheap rate, and hence traditional banks' entire business model would become outdated and obsolete. It would be like them trying to sell video tapes and old-school film cameras in the world of online video streaming, digital cameras, and smart phones. Or, like using pigeon post in the age of instant messaging. Yes, people used to do that… And it was the standard… But guess what? The world is changing… fast!

We can keep listing examples that validate the point of technological disruption all day. But let's move on with the main story. In the presence of countless young, ambitious, and dynamic fintech startups, we would just like to remind our dear friends in banking of this old saying: don't bring a knife to a gunfight!

So, why would we expect that fewer people will be depositing their money with traditional banks in the future?

Until now, there were very few places where people could store their money. One option was to keep it at home and have jars filled with banknotes, bury piles of cash in the garden, or simply deposit funds in the bank where money may be safer than at home, provided the bank doesn't go bust, of course. Another advantage is that bank transfers made it easy to send money to other people or companies.

But how about the billions of people around the world who have been ignored forever by traditional banks and basically cut out of the financial system? If old-school banks don't want to serve them, somebody else will do! Fintech is coming and blockchain is leading the way!

The advent of Bitcoin and other cryptoassets gave people a viable alternative. You already know that blockchain enables secure payments and store of value without third-party interference. Whatever digital money you have on the blockchain, it will be there, and nobody can take it away, provided you store your private keys properly. Therefore, banks aren't the only option for storing your funds anymore. The most clear evidence that people consider cryptoassets as a viable alternative comes from countries suffering hyperinflation, like the recent examples with Zimbabwe and Venezuela. The price of Bitcoin skyrocketed there and held a substantial premium over the rest of the world. This was due to the exceptionally high demand for Bitcoin in these countries.

In addition, transactions carried out on the blockchain tend to be much faster and cheaper compared to traditional bank transfers, especially international ones. In the future, new solutions will emerge and current solutions will be improved significantly. So, any kinds of money transfers will likely be way more efficient, cheaper, and faster than existing payment systems.

All of this will likely benefit consumers and disrupt traditional banks, as they start losing business to the more effective and efficient fintech startups.

Of course, traditional banks can choose how to address the upcoming technological disruption. We believe that the smart response would be to try and adapt to the changing paradigm and embrace new technology with all the benefits it brings. You can't stop progress! And it would be foolish to ignore it or try to resist to it. Whoever chooses to be rigid or otherwise fails to adapt to the new environment risks exemplifying yet another confirmation of the principle of evolution and follow the fate of the dinosaurs, or of Blockbuster, the former movie rental giant of 15 years ago, which was displaced by services such as Netflix.

Next, we'll examine how blockchain solutions can impact some of the existing services offered by traditional banks.

Banking business lines that can be potentially disrupted

Besides the obvious risk of deposit outflows, there are several other ways in which blockchain can transform different areas of banking.

In this section, we will discuss blockchain's impact on various banking functions, which are listed in the following diagram:

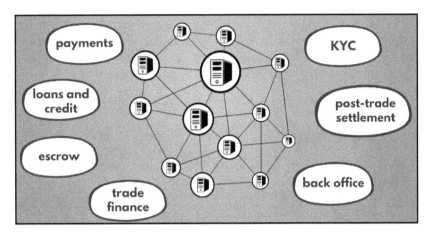

This isn't a short list, but all of the topics are really interesting. So, let's get started.

Billions of dollars are paid in banking fees each day. Some of these fees are clearly shown to customers and are for services rendered, while others are less obvious and arise when banks carry out operations related to foreign exchange, for example.

It has been reported that global banks such as Santander are very reliant on fees from international money transfers. An internal document that leaked in 2017 showed that such fees accounted for no less than 10% of Santander's revenue in 2016.

On the other hand, once some blockchain-based solutions become mainstream, they could provide superior options for such transactions. Blockchain-based money transfers take less time, and do not cost nearly as much as traditional bank transfers. Currently (at this early stage of the technology), Bitcoin takes a few minutes to a few hours to process a payment, while international bank transfers usually take at least three working days to settle. Other blockchains, such as Ethereum, Litecoin, Ripple, and Stellar, enable even faster and cheaper transactions, which can provide huge savings compared to the amount of time and fees it takes banks to do the same. And some improvements to these protocols, such as the lightning network, can provide even more efficiency. So, national and especially international money transfers are a service that will likely be disrupted.

In Chapter 3, *The Birth of Bitcoin and the Advantages of a Decentralized Payment System*, we discussed the reasons why bank transfers are still so complicated, time consuming, and expensive. They involve multiple intermediate steps, such as working with correspondent banks, and can suffer from long lines, exchange rate losses, counter-party risks, bureaucracy, and extensive paperwork. Blockchain solutions circumvent all these difficulties and are carried out on a peer-to-peer basis without the involvement of third parties. Naturally, this makes the process much cheaper and faster:

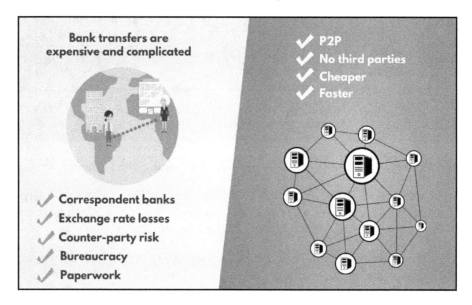

Some banking incumbents have shown that they are aware of the potential disruption and are taking steps towards implementing blockchain solutions for international money transfers.

A consortium of ANZ Bank, BNP Paribas, BNY Mellon, Wells Fargo, and Hyperledger developers have completed a **proof of concept** (**POC**) for cross-border payments built with the Hyperledger Fabric blockchain platform. It is designed to test whether moving member bank accounts to a distributed ledger could help the interbank payments platform SWIFT reconcile in real time. Hyperledger Fabric enables real-time visibility on the liquidity of Nostro accounts, simplifying reconciliation and allowing liquidity savings while meeting key industry requirements such as governance, data privacy, standardization, and identity management.

Separately, in September 2017, the **Royal Bank of Canada** (**RBC**) started using Hyperledger for its US-Canada interbank settlements.

Now, let's move on to the next line of business. The deposit taking and credit giving model consists of two parts. We already discussed the deposit side. Now, let's talk about lending and the transformation it could experience in the future.

How blockchain can affect lending

Today, banks continue to be the main source of credit to people and companies. Peer-to-peer lending is a popular niche, but informational asymmetries impede its implementation on a large scale. P2P lending relies on a solid idea. If people deposit their funds in banks and then banks use their customers' money to lend it to other people, doesn't it make more sense for depositors to lend their money directly to borrowers and earn a higher rate of return on their money? Banks seem to be the redundant middleman in this equation, don't they? Their main added value comes from the fact that they arguably have expertise in sorting out good from bad borrowers, and also specialize in dealing with bad debtors once they stop servicing their debt.

It is more than likely that in the future platforms involving smart contracts will make things easier and more transparent. Informational asymmetries between borrowers and lenders can be reduced due to the clarity deriving from the blockchain. Pre-agreed terms will be respected and there will be some sort of public database, in which people will be able to see who has been a good borrower in the past and lend them money:

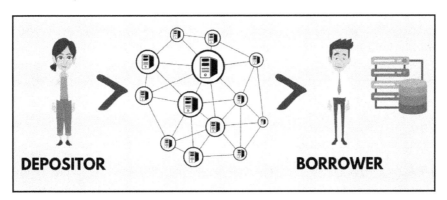

Think of an online marketplace. Sellers and buyers in such marketplaces have ratings. Reputation is the very foundation for being successful in the long run.

Well, imagine a world where borrowers will have reputations and all of their previous relevant actions will be recorded on the blockchain. This would certainly reduce informational asymmetries. Lenders would have more information regarding the type of borrower they are about to lend money to. Moreover, this information would be immutable and easily accessible. This would create a competitive market where lending services are easily accessible to people because they are less expensive and faster. Banks are burdened by huge administrative costs, which inflate the final interest rates they charge borrowers. In a P2P lending market facilitated by blockchain and smart contract technology, lenders wouldn't have to cover nearly as many admin costs and would be happy to receive a fraction of the interest rates charged by banks.

Another area blockchain will likely disrupt is trade finance and escrow services. In the world of today, there are many parties trading with each other, but not trusting one another. Banks help reduce such asymmetries by providing letters of credit and escrow services.

Think of a retailer in Europe who wants to import clothes from China. He has managed to find a factory producing clothes and they provide a good price for the first shipment. Its total value is 500,000 euros, which is not a negligible sum. The problem is that the retailer hasn't worked with the supplier so far and cannot be certain that the Chinese manufacturer will deliver the clothes once the money has been sent. At the same time, the Chinese manufacturer doesn't have a guarantee the European retailer will send the money once the goods have been shipped. Sounds like an impasse, doesn't it?

Well, the solution that has been established, as of now, is to use an escrow account. The European retailer will deposit the funds in a trusted bank, which will then release the funds only when the producer has shipped the goods. In this case, the bank's reputation removes informational asymmetries on both sides and facilitates the trade. The bank guarantees with its name and regulatory license that the process will be as legitimate as possible. However, banks charge a percentage of the total transaction value for this service.

Platforms based on smart contracts could transform this line of business.

The two parties in a business transaction will be able to design a mechanism that transfers title to goods and money automatically. The conditions according to which the deal will take place will be programmed into a smart contract and both parties can be certain that these are immutable and will be executed automatically.

As you can see, plenty of exciting changes are coming our way. But there is more!

In the current environment, banks have to engage in KYC processes. Authorities all over the world expect from banks to collect information about their customers and verify their identity. The aim of these regulations is to prevent money laundering and impede financing of crime and terrorist organizations. As you can probably imagine, this is a lengthy process. Some banks work with millions of clients and they have to fill in tons of forms and investigate any suspicious cases. This is a significant investment on their part. Every bank has to go through this process when it starts working with a new client of a certain size.

A much more efficient way to do this would be to organize a unique distributed database, which can be shared among banks and regulators. In this way, they would be able to save themselves all the research effort that has already been carried out by their colleagues. A distributed blockchain solution would be optimal for these purposes, given that the immutability of records means client transaction history is stored in a secure and unbiased manner by all banks who share such blockchain platform. It would also increase transparency, but only to entities who have permissioned access, as we believe such a solution is most viable to be implemented as a private permissioned blockchain.

Actually, such solutions are already being developed and tested; here are a couple of examples.

In 2017, only 44% of Filipinos were utilizing bank accounts, a metric that is quickly increasing thanks to rapid economic growth in the Philippines, but is still hampered by inefficient mechanisms for checking the identity and history of new account applicants. KYC laws require asking for the same data over and over, much of which is not available in digital or verifiable form.

To solve this, the Bankers Association of the Philippines, in partnership with Hyperledger and a coalition of major banks, undertook a proof-of-concept exercise to build a prototype that implements identity verification using Hyperledger Indy.

The platform streamlines the onboarding of new accounts by allowing customers to enter information only once in a privacy-preserving way, and reuse that data for new account opening. Banks can trust that the history of that data is solid. If successful, this could serve as a test for a nationwide ID system.

In October 2017, another similar initiative by a consortium of a Singapore regulator and several banks, including HSBC and Mitsubishi UFJ, announced that they have completed a proof-of-concept for a KYC blockchain. The functionality, scalability, and security of the prototype were tested between February and May 2017. Results showed that the blockchain functioned well even with a high volume of information flow. It proved to be tamper-resistant to third-party intervention, while securing confidentiality by only allowing access to those with legitimate authentication.

Similarly, banks' back offices will have a much easier time when blockchain is implemented in the context of post-trade settlement. An improved process trusted by both counterparties will reduce settlement times because both sides share and have control over the same distributed ledger system and can be certain that the prearranged conditions are preserved. Moreover, there will be fewer mechanical errors deriving from system failure. All market participants could share the same automated settlement system on the blockchain. Of course, all of this will lead to audit and reconciliation efficiencies too. Individual parties involved in each trade will not have to do unnecessary replication of records and perform audits to ensure overall consistency. Ultimately, banks will be able to have leaner and less expensive back office structures, which will work much faster.

OK, great! These are some of the impacts blockchain technology is expected to have on the traditional banking business. Next, we'll present a case study about trade finance and blockchain.

Trade finance on the blockchain

Now, we'll have a look at a specific initiative by IBM and several global banks, which goes on to highlight what we discussed in the previous sections. Innovation in traditional finance is already underway.

The specific initiative we will examine is called **Batavia**, and it involves a partnership between IBM and UBS, joined by several other major banks such as Bank of Montreal, CaixaBank, Commerzbank, and Erste Group. Its main goal is to tackle the inefficient processes in the field of trade finance.

Trade finance is a slow process burdened by bureaucracy, as it stands now: a lengthy process involving multiple verifications carried out by different participants. In most cases, a single deal involves a buyer, a seller, a buyer's bank, a seller's bank, a transportation company, and local authorities. The entire process requires plenty of paperwork and isn't automated because all participants have their own separate IT systems, which require human intervention for reconciliation and verification:

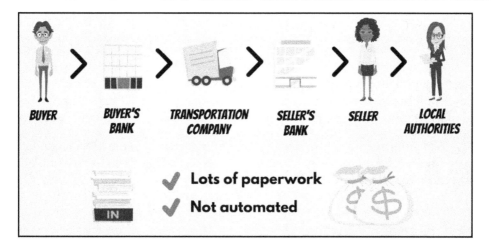

The process is lengthy (taking weeks in some cases) and expensive for companies (given that they have to pay man-hours and can't use the proceeds of the deal in the meantime).

Therefore, a trade finance platform like Batavia definitely makes sense and feels like a breath of fresh air. Companies will be able to use the platform to enter into agreements with each other using standard forms. What is even more important is that the degree of transparency and trust in the system will increase due to its secure and immutable distributed ledger.

The platform is designed in a very innovative way. All parties involved will be able to track the status and whereabouts of the goods exchanged. Another key feature is that money can be paid to different participants in the trade at different stages, as goods move along the supply chain:

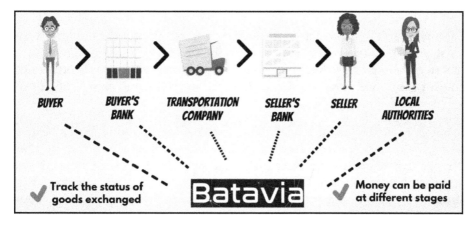

For example, a company will be able to pay its supplier once goods are in the hands of the logistics firm. Then the logistics firm will be paid once the shipment arrives at its destination.

Batavia is an open platform encouraging companies, banks, and authorities to join forces together and collaborate towards a more efficient outcome for all. Such initiatives promote trade and make it more efficient, thereby creating value and stimulating economic growth.

This is a great example of a platform that has been constructed using blockchain technology and can potentially disrupt the existing status quo in trade finance by increasing efficiency and effectiveness for all parties involved.

Blockchain and insurance

The insurance industry doesn't seem to be as vulnerable to technological disruption as traditional banking. Insurance is a highly specialized business where risk assessment and the ability to pool a large number of insurance contracts with similar risk profiles is a critical success factor that is difficult, but not impossible, to replicate automatically in a decentralized P2P marketplace. Hence, P2P and decentralized insurance underwriting are way more complex to implement than traditional banking.

On the other hand, the advent of blockchain technology represents a potentially great source of efficiency and innovation for insurers. And this time, the incumbents are not too late for the party!

Some insurance companies are already taking advantage of blockchain technology to position their businesses for success and increase profitability.

For example, Allianz demonstrated a beta version of a platform facilitating the settlement of catastrophe swaps and bonds. Such a platform makes it easier for the holders of such financial instruments to receive or send a payoff, in the case of a triggering event. This means a shorter waiting time for both parties, less uncertainty for people buying these instruments for insurance purposes, fewer verification errors, and an overall improved customer experience.

Lloyd's in the UK has not waited too long and started experimenting with blockchain-based products already. It partnered with the shared workspace provider Vrumi and blockchain digital specialist SafeShare to offer insurance products to Vrumi's hosts. Vrumi is an AirBnB-style company for office space accommodation and the idea is to allow Vrumi's hosts to underwrite insurance contracts protecting their rented property. The product uses blockchain technology to confirm and execute the obligations of each party.

And do you remember Everledger, the company that uses blockchain to track the origin of diamonds? It also helps insurers when pricing related insurance products by mitigating the risk of fraud and blood diamonds entering the supply chain. Purchased diamonds typically come with a certificate to prove their quality and origin but there is a history of fraud from missing paperwork. Blockchain could greatly help insurers when they need to verify the history of diamonds, works of art, jewelry, and luxury goods by preventing any fraud attempts.

There are a number of blockchain applications that will shape the development of the insurance industry in the future. For now, we know that blockchain can help by doing the following:

- Reducing uncertainty
- Lowering back-office costs and reducing bureaucracy
- Automating pay-off execution processes, saving time and man-power
- Improving customer relationships and satisfaction since blockchain-based smart contracts are objective and pre-programmed to execute automatically

Moreover, insurance contracts on the blockchain can help insurers improve their capital adequacy ratios due to better risk management, faster execution times, and improved visibility over pay-offs due to policy holders.

Overall, the main industry feeling is that permissioned blockchains can be a great solution for the future of the insurance sector. Such permissioned blockchains can fit into the current business model. If blockchain solutions are integrated with the existing framework, insurers, regulators, and customers can all benefit from the advantages discussed here.

Investment banking and blockchain

Earlier in this chapter, we said that there are two types of banking, commercial and investment banking. We discussed the potential impact of blockchain technology on traditional commercial banking services, but we didn't say much about investment banking.

We'll do that briefly in this section.

Investment banks typically have the following core business lines:

- **Capital markets**: Issuing stocks and bonds to raise capital for their corporate clients on the primary market, selling them to investors, and trading them on the secondary market for clients or for the bank's own account
- **Advisory services**: Consulting companies in times of specialized processes such as mergers and acquisitions, as well as corporate restructuring
- **Asset management**: Managing clients' funds professionally in an investment portfolio

OK, let's examine each of these areas one by one.

Capital markets are all about raising capital for companies in the form of equity or debt. It's not hard to imagine that equity and debt securities can be represented by tokens on the blockchain and issued and traded there. In fact, this could be a much more efficient way to do that, as clearing and settlement can be done directly and almost instantaneously, rather than waiting several days and paying fees to a bunch of intermediaries.

Here's a real example of a pilot project for a bond trading platform developed by Hyperledger Sawtooth. They identified the issues with legacy systems as follows:

- Record keeping practices differ between institutions and reconciling ledgers is often difficult, expensive, and time consuming
- Historical bond ownership data can be fractured and incomplete
- Centralized data management solutions have monopolized their offerings
- Data can be altered retroactively, leading to financial fraud
- Centralized systems risk single points of failure

To streamline the process of transferring bonds, Hyperledger Sawtooth created a user interface and smart contract platform that allow investors to track and transfer bonds in real time. Here, users can create, buy, sell, and settle their portfolio of bonds. While the smart contracts were customized specifically for bonds and their unique identifiers, they can be tailored accordingly to a wide range of financial instruments.

There are many advantages to migrate financial markets to the blockchain. It promotes data consistency across different market participants. It helps maintain comprehensive, ordered, accurate, and immutable records of historical ownership. In addition, decentralization, transparency, and trust are inherent in the system.

Naturally, this can be extended to any type of financial instruments used for capital raising or risk hedging. Smart contracts can be very useful to structure any kind of derivatives or other exotic financial products that are traded on global capital markets.

In the future, all established financial markets platforms could be migrated to blockchains as they provide a more efficient financial infrastructure. Actually, this future may come sooner than most people expect…

In July 2017, London Stock Exchange Group, in a partnership with IBM, announced that it will create a blockchain platform designed for digitally issuing shares of Italian companies. Hyperledger Fabric will form the basis of the platform.

NASDAQ has also been very active in developing blockchain trading platforms.

The **Australian Securities Exchange** (**ASX**) has announced that it will replace its current clearing system with blockchain technology.

And the list goes on… global capital markets are moving to blockchain.

Besides efficiencies to established financial markets, blockchain also provides access to the new emerging cryptoasset class.

Interestingly, some major financial institutions, such as Goldman Sachs, Barclays, and Fidelity, among others, have been exploring opening cryptoasset trading desks. It seems that this new asset class soon may find its place next to traditional asset classes on banks' trading floors.

In advisory services, the blockchain impact is a little bit more far-fetched, as the space is so new, companies are very early-stage and mostly fall below the radar of established investment banks.

What about blockchain and asset management? This area is moving ahead quite dynamically too. The new cryptoasset class, led by Bitcoin, is emerging and gaining recognition among asset managers worldwide. The interest among institutional and retail investors alike is growing strong, and the offering of related investment products is following closely the market demand. Bitcoin futures were launched on two of the largest global commodity exchanges in Chicago, CME and CBOE, at the end of 2017. NASDAQ is planning to launch a similar product too. Bitcoin and Ethereum Exchange Traded Notes are listed in Sweden. A Bitcoin Investment Trust, sponsored by Grayscale, is also available to qualified investors. And Bitcoin Exchange Traded Funds (or ETFs) on the New York Stock Exchange have been in the pipeline, but it seems more time is needed for such product to come to fruition. This is just the beginning and the way ahead is long and uncertain, but also exciting. Cryptoassets are extremely hard to value, so we'll see how the space evolves, but one thing is clear: the asset management industry is moving in a direction where cryptoassets will play an increasingly important role. So, we can expect that new exciting developments are in the making!

Blockchain and financial regulation

The rise of blockchain and cryptoassets in 2017 caused significant headaches to regulators around the world. Price volatility, significant interest from retail and institutional investors alike, the launch of Bitcoin futures on major regulated exchanges, along with a daily presence in mainstream media meant cryptoassets are becoming validated as a new asset class of their own.

In the traditional finance world, regulators oversee financial markets to make sure there are adequate rules in place that balance the interests of all parties involved. On one hand, they need to protect retail investors (private individuals) who are considered potentially vulnerable due to lack of experience and expertise in evaluating market risk and making investment decisions. On the other hand, regulators should also help maintain efficient and orderly capital markets that allow companies to raise enough capital to fund their operations, boost innovation, and ultimately stimulate the economy. This makes the job of financial regulators a really important and demanding one. They need to constantly keep up with new types of financial engineering and sometimes exotic structures and instruments like various financial derivative products and their risk profiles. They need to constantly keep a watchful eye on publicly traded corporations and institutional investors for potential mischief by their management, which can involve false accounting, insider or otherwise rogue trading, Ponzi or pyramid schemes, or other regulatory violations. The list of examples in history is really long and the creativity of people when money is on the line is unlimited. We already mentioned earlier some huge multi-billion-dollar scandals involving Enron, WorldCom, Bernie Madoff, and pretty much all major banks. Moreover, regulators need to be especially careful with large financial enterprises that can represent systemic risk, meaning that if they get in trouble this could endanger the entire financial and economic system.

So, you can see that financial regulators have a huge responsibility and an important social mandate. Naturally, as the cryptoasset market is getting bigger, it has started to attract their attention. The open question now is how the balance between upholding investor protection and keeping technological innovation unhampered can be preserved once again. And here, this is a very challenging task because blockchain cryptoassets are at the forefront of technology, finance, economics, and legal science at the same time.

Certainly, the unsophisticated investor public needs to be protected. Just like in any other market, there are fraud and scams being perpetrated. These things, unfortunately, have always been part of society. There is also irresponsible behavior by market participants who have difficulty understanding the risks involved.

Well, the good news is that the cryptoassets market is not considered to pose systemic risk. This is the common view among central banks around the world right now. This is due to its very small size compared to the global equity and debt markets.

How cryptoassets are treated in the existing regulatory framework, given the mix of currency, commodity, and equity features they appear to have, is a totally different and complex question. On one side, everybody has heard of cryptocurrencies and uses this term to refer to the entire cryptoasset space. But they don't account for all currencies. Actually, commodities may be closer in their nature to the cryptoassets, out of all the established asset classes. This is because their market value is determined by supply and demand for the utility or use case they enable. And this should be the case with many cryptoassets too. For example, the Ethereum tokens give access to the computational power of the Ethereum network and to data storage on the secure, immutable Ethereum blockchain. This looks like a real use case, similar to many commodities in our modern economy. Think about oil, electricity, and cargo or freight; these are all tradable commodities with substantial utility in the modern economy. Perhaps, Ethereum and some of its blockchain peers will follow suit. And what about Bitcoin? It is gaining the widely recognized status of digital gold. Its utility, as a store of value, is similar to a certain extent to that of gold. The **Chicago Mercantile Exchange** (or **CME**), one of the largest regulated financial and commodity derivative exchanges in the world, seems to share this view, evidenced by its listing of Bitcoin futures contracts in December 2017.

In contrast, the value of equities is fundamentally underpinned by the stream of future cash flows the underlying business is expected to realize. This is not necessarily the case with most cryptoassets at present. Of course, traditional equity shares can be represented by tokens on the blockchain, as we already mentioned. This can be done with pretty much any asset.

And how about the venture capital aspect of cryptoassets, which at present mostly represent stakeholder interest in start-up projects? And by stakeholder here, we mean anyone with any interest in a venture or ecosystem. For example, the primary stakeholders in a typical corporation are its investors, employees, customers, and suppliers.

The status of cryptoassets in the current market and regulatory landscape is an open and complex topic, which we, by no means, can cover completely here.

We'll just mention that when it comes to cryptoassets, the global regulatory environment is very diverse and is evolving dynamically. Some countries are more conservative, while others are more open and liberal, just like with any other economic and political developments. The reasonable approach would probably be to have ongoing dialog between regulators and market participants, so that everyone is on the same page and contributes towards an efficient outcome for society. It seems that many regulators and government authorities recognize the value of blockchain technology and want to get a good understanding of it before further steps are taken. This approach makes sense and we can see some positive initiatives already taking place.

In April 2018, 22 countries in the European Union signed a declaration on the Establishment of a European Blockchain Partnership.

Mariya Gabriel, the Commissioner for Digital Economy and Society, was the person who promoted the partnership and stated that she believes in the technology's potential to transform the digital world:

> *"In the future, all public services will use blockchain technology. Blockchain is a great opportunity for Europe and Member States to rethink their information systems, to promote user trust and the protection of personal data, to help create new business opportunities and to establish new areas of leadership, benefiting citizens, public services and companies. The Partnership enables Member States to work together with the European Commission to turn the enormous potential of blockchain technology into better services for citizens."*

This partnership will be a vehicle for cooperation among EU Member States to exchange experience and expertise in technical and regulatory fields and prepare for the launch of EU-wide blockchain applications across the Digital Single Market for the benefit of the public and private sectors. This will contribute to Europe continuing to play a leading role in the development and rollout of blockchain technologies.

With that said, we'll leave the regulatory conundrum open, and encourage everyone to be reasonable and try and understand blockchain technology for themselves before taking any action. Actually, this is exactly the aim of this book and we'll be extremely happy if we can contribute to the ongoing discussion and increase social awareness of blockchain technology.

Blockchain and the retail sector

Now, let's move on to the potential impact of blockchain technology on the retail industry. But first, we'll discuss a term that has been previously mentioned in this book.

The Internet of Things

IoT, which is how the **Internet of Things** is frequently referred to, is a concept that describes the interconnectivity through the internet of different devices we use in our daily lives.

We don't simply access the internet from a computer anymore. There are different smart devices surrounding us that have built-in functionalities based on the internet and are connected with other devices or the cloud:

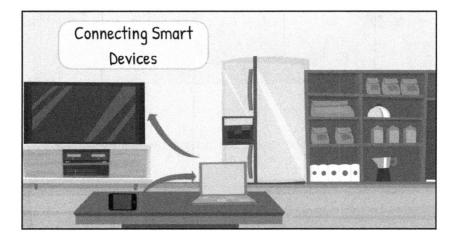

We all know what smart TVs and smart phones are. Nowadays, many appliances are being produced with smart functionalities, such as air conditioners that are connected with smartphones and track people's location to turn themselves on when you come home from work. Security systems connected with the internet notifying you if a suspicious event is registered at your home. And the list goes on:

Wearable devices are at the heart of the most recent discussions of the IoT and the retail industry. And one of the first implementations of such wearable devices is security and identification. This, without a doubt, means that blockchain technology can play an important role in this field:

Many people wear badges at work, and these provide security, identification, and in some cases valuable insights related to location (which can be extremely helpful for security reasons). It isn't an intuitive idea, but the badge itself is some sort of a smart device playing a role in the IoT. The chip it contains provides information about its holder, about his or her position, and any type of relevant data that has been stored in the system. Modern badges are even more secure, they require holders to use biometric identifications such as fingerprint or eye scan:

How is this related to the retail industry?

Well, this goes on to show you that a simple chip inserted in a product can contain vast amounts of information. And if the information contained in this chip is recorded on the blockchain, it becomes immutable and unforgeable:

In the same way, such chips can be added to most retail products.

It is likely that many clothes, footwear, bags, perfumes, sun glasses, cosmetics, luxury goods, medicines, and so on will benefit from a transparent authenticity verification platform that will have scale and will be mass adopted. This would allow customers to scan footwear (through a barcode or a chip inserted inside) and receive valuable information about the product. They could be interested in learning the item's true producer, the country of origin, the source of materials and labor used, when the item was produced, and possibly the recommended price from its producer. This could help remedy unethical practices such as sweatshops and child labor in some developing countries:

Moreover, famous brands such as Nike suffer from a lot of counterfeiting. And the problem is that customers are not always able to distinguish Nike's original products from imitations. A blockchain-based verification process could help solve this issue:

Nowadays, consumers have become very conscious about health, and the social impact of their actions, and they prefer consuming products that have been produced the right way.

In this context, the perspective of blockchain-powered verification and proof of authenticity becomes extremely useful:

Consumers will be able to confirm the authenticity of the products they purchase. Gradually, unethical manufacturing practices and the market for counterfeit goods could shrink significantly.

This is even more critical for cosmetics, medicines, and other healthcare products, because quality of production and adherence to standards are not only desired, but vital. A public blockchain-based registry could assure people that the medicines they buy have been produced by legit companies with solid reputations, under the right conditions and standards, and using appropriate ingredients. With such transparency, producers stand behind their products with their reputation and license to operate and can be held accountable for bringing a faulty product to the market or breaking the rules otherwise:

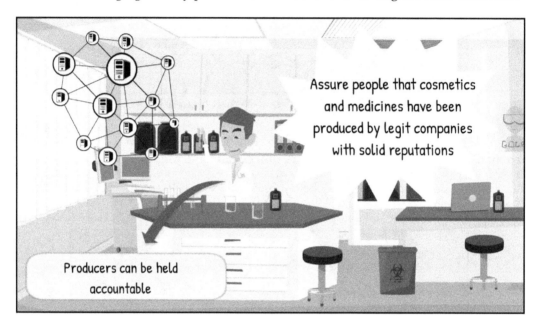

Such a registry would allow consumers to verify the entire life cycle of the products they buy. From a social standpoint, it would be possible to show consumers that the clothes they wear have been produced in an adequate environment and certified by organizations verifying the decency of workplace conditions. And this is really important for a large part of the consumer population in our day and age. They want to know more about the products they use and are interested in their life cycle.

Importantly, when buying fashion products or cosmetics, customers want to know when an item has been produced. They don't want to be sold goods that have been produced a year ago. So, such a type of certification would be useful from this perspective as well:

Customers will be able to verify how long ago a product has been produced

Blockchain and intellectual property

Now, let's see the potential impact of blockchain on media downloads such as music or films, software installations, and other products that have to do with **intellectual property (IP)**.

Intellectual property management is another field where the implementation of blockchain-based solutions could have an important impact. IP is a hot topic in the internet age.

By using a distributed ledger to manage IP rights, artists, authors, and businesses can have tamper-proof evidence of ownership of their IP and copyright protection. They can also use smart contracts in an ecosystem that allows smart IP rights management.

Let's consider what each of these developments means separately:

One of the most important aspects when talking about IP rights is their registration and protection. In most legislations, IP rights, trademarks, and copyrights are valid from the moment of their inception. A blockchain-based registry with timestamps that show when an IP right has been generated could represent a proof of first use. This would make it much more difficult for vulture firms to file for patents for technologies that have been created and used by their original authors but have not been registered yet by them. A timestamp on the blockchain's immutable ledger would be a transparent and convincing proof to the whole world of the rightful IP ownership.

Blockchain-based solutions open a world of possibilities for IP-related products such as music, films, software, and pretty much any form of authorship.

First of all, blockchain platforms would facilitate content creators and artists to monetize their work in a decentralized system based on digital money and smart contracts. It would be possible to build systems and frameworks triggering automatic IP payments based on usage with great precision. For example, music and video streaming could be charged by the minute or even the second with micro-payments being processed instantaneously. As in the other industries we've discussed so far, these systems could work in a direct peer-to-peer way, without any unnecessary intermediaries.

Kodak's launch of a blockchain-based platform registering photo image rights and triggering automatic payments to authors whenever their images have been used is a great example of such an initiative. Smart contracts make the whole process much faster, more secure, and more efficient. Such solutions could be especially effective in situations where a little-known artist creates a product and needs to rely on a third-party platform to protect his or her IP rights.

Similarly to Steemit, which we mentioned earlier, the StreamSpace project aims to build a decentralized platform governed by its community of content creators and users. The main idea here is that the centralized model, in which monopolies such as Netflix and Amazon decide how much to charge customers and what percentage of royalties to pay to authors, is not optimal for the latter. StreamSpace offers authors the independence to choose their commercial strategy on their own and charge customers using StreamShare tokens:

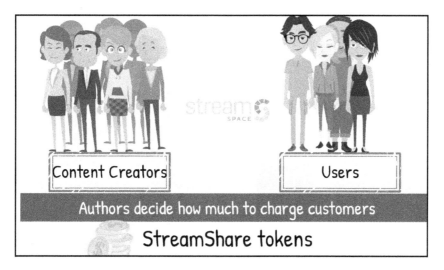

Another project, **Dot Blockchain Media** (**dotBC**) is building a music content rights registry that will help musicians express their rights and wishes in commercializing their art in an interoperable file format. Data is maintained across a distributed network that utilizes Hyperledger Sawtooth blockchain technology. This solution integrates the record keeping of music and media rights into the works of artists themselves. dotBC maintains partnerships in the music and wider media industries to enable seamless data exchanges between more than 63 million globally recorded works from independent and major label artists and the dotBC ecosystem.

It remains to be seen how such decentralized marketplaces will develop in the future and whether they will reach a critical mass of users. One of the main challenges ahead of them is the governance model of a decentralized community of disparate stakeholders, which is, in fact, a common issue for all decentralized systems:

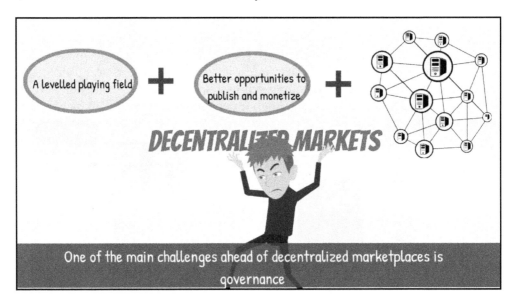

One of the main challenges ahead of decentralized marketplaces is governance

However, thanks to blockchain technology, we will likely see a significant disruption in the way artists manage their intellectual property. Chances are the playing field will be more level in the future, and artists will have better opportunities to publish, distribute, and monetize their content on their own in an environment that also protects their IP rights.

Blockchain and the food sector

We have already mentioned several times that blockchain can provide great improvements and efficiencies to the food industry supply chain, and to pretty much any supply chain, for that matter. But since the food we consume is such an essential part of our daily lives with vital implications, and the food industry is such a big part of the global economy, we will focus on it here and analyze how blockchain technology can help deliver better outcomes for everyone. In fact, many of the food industry leaders of today have already recognized this and are launching pilot projects and initiatives to implement blockchain solutions in their business models. We'll examine some case studies of such projects here:

We'll start with a very important question. Do you like fish? Whoever does knows how important it is for fish to be delivered and served fresh.

The issues in the traditional seafood industry supply chain include illegal fishing practices, mislabeling fraud, improper food storage conditions, and laborious and error-prone manual record keeping:

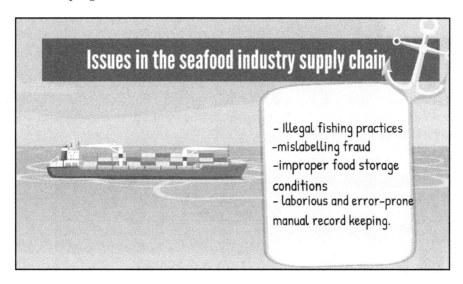

These problems negatively impact producers, retailers, consumers, the world's natural resources, and the economy as a whole:

The following is a blockchain project aiming to resolve all this:

Intel is building a blockchain solution using Hyperledger technology to implement a modern approach to seafood traceability. Leveraging the Hyperledger Sawtooth framework, the seafood journey can now be recorded from ocean to table. IoT sensors can be attached to any seafood that is entrusted to someone else for transport, with trackable ownership, possession, and telemetry parameters such as location, temperature, humidity, motion, shock, and title. The final buyer can access a complete record of information and trust that it is accurate:

A blockchain-operated seafood supply chain can help prevent fish caught illegally or stored improperly from entering the market. It can level the playing field for suppliers and reward good practices. Vendors and consumers will know what they're getting and get what they're paying for. Therefore, blockchain can increase transparency and trust throughout the system. Moreover, smart contract automation can save time and operating costs.

Another huge proponent of blockchain technology is none other than Walmart. And again, the application is focused on the food supply chain.

Big retailers like Walmart have suffered along with consumers from contaminated food entering the market on many occasions. To realize the seriousness this problem, consider the following example.

A decade ago in the United States, a deadly strain of E. coli in tainted spinach ripped through 26 states, killing three people and sickening more than 200. The outbreak showed what can happen when sourcing food and tracing contamination goes horribly wrong:

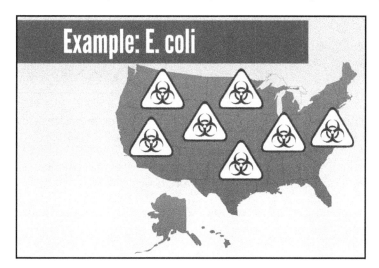

The case was described by Walmart executives as follows: "Consumers, in general, stopped eating spinach. Restaurants pulled it off the menu. If you could track and pinpoint where that came from faster, you could alleviate all that and ensure consumer confidence continues":

This is not an isolated instance. Over the years, there have been multiple cases of food safety issues on a large scale.

The 2017 Salmonella outbreak in the US linked to papayas from Mexico resulted in 235 people falling ill, out of which 2 died and 78 were hospitalized.

You also probably remember the notorious 2008 scandal in China with infant formula mixed with melamine, a toxic chemical:

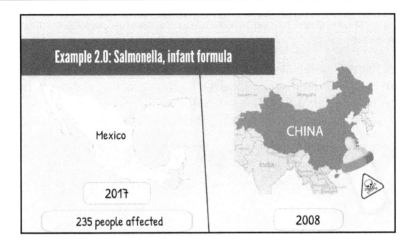

And the list goes on…

So, let's see the solution Walmart is implementing.

As a pilot project, it teamed up with IBM and Tsinghua University in Beijing to digitally track the movement of pork in China on a blockchain. For that purpose, they are using Hyperledger technology. It will enable retailers to track the movement of meat from producers to processors, to distributors, to grocers, and finally to consumers:

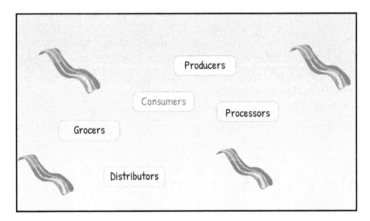

According to IBM, this initiative represents a substantial improvement over earlier projects that solely used barcodes and radio ID tags.

The missing piece was a shared forum where companies could see each others' transactions and develop trust. That missing piece is something like the blockchain.

Information to be stored on the blockchain, where fraud and inaccuracies are much harder to get away with, includes details related to farm origins, factory data, expiration dates, storage temperatures, and shipping. Blockchain technology can substantially streamline the industry supply chain and promote material efficiencies over the legacy model:

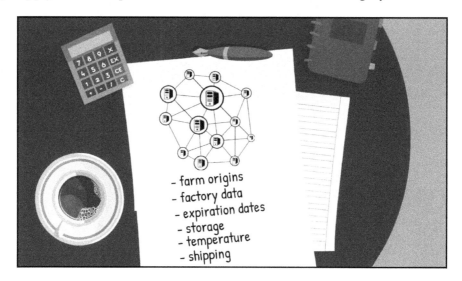

Given the great promise of this pilot project, Walmart has subsequently expanded it to include more food products. Other consumer staples giants, such as Nestlé, Unilever, and Dole, have also joined the initiative. It seems that everybody in the space likes the idea of improving supply chains with automatic tracking of important information, such as temperature and quality of goods, shipment and delivery dates, and safety certifications of facilities.

Blockchain and the transportation sector

Mobility services and the business of automotive companies in general will probably be one of the most vibrant and radically transformed sectors in the years to come. Traditional carmakers such as Volkswagen, Toyota, and GM face two main types of challenges over the next decade.

First, they have to adapt to a product line, which will be less reliant on traditional fuels, and focused on electric batteries. This is a significant change of pace and global car producers have no choice but to adapt their business models, or competitors like Tesla will continue to gain market share.

The other main business risk for auto producers is the threat posed by firms such as Uber, Lyft, and Didi. Well, this can also be an opportunity; depends on how you look at it.

The first type of challenge, the transition from traditional fuel to electric batteries has little to do with blockchain technology. At least, if we don't get into the supply chain.

The other challenge: the way people are changing their transportation behavior and the way they consume mobility services is what we would like to discuss here. A significant number of innovative solutions in this space could be blockchain-based.

Most large car producers experiment with some sort of car sharing, ride sharing, or hailing schemes. For example, a few years ago, Daimler introduced Car2Go, a short-term car rental service, which allows people to hop in a car and use it for transportation from point A to point B. The flexibility to leave a transportation vehicle on the street feels like a change of paradigm for many people living in big cities. It is hard, and frankly next to impossible, to find a parking space during peak hours in places such as New York, London, Hong Kong, Paris, Tokyo, Shanghai, and many others. It is much more convenient economically to use a car for a limited amount of time and then pass it on to the next user who needs it. And it is not only Daimler experimenting with such smart vehicle sharing schemes. Another example is the collaboration between Fiat and the oil producer Eni in Italy. Their joint venture is called **Enjoy** and it offers a similar service. Most automakers need to adapt to this new business model, or they risk losing market share. On one hand, they see car sharing as a threat because it means that not every individual needs to buy and maintain a personal vehicle. On the other hand though, it can be seen also as an opportunity because car sharing can allow these companies to build subscription-based businesses. This could make up for the lost revenue in traditional segments and could even create more value.

In the future, blockchain technology can play a key role in expanding car sharing services in the global economy. Blockchain-based solutions can help car sharing service providers verify drivers' identities, driving histories, and previous car-sharing usage. This could help mitigate certain risks with greater precision based on the risk profiles of individual drivers. Smart contracts can enable automatic payments related to toll road fees, and insurance contracts that could be adjusted according to the driver's profile and the distance he or she travels. They can also be used for automatic payments for cleaning, refueling, and other services during the journey. Such automation would boost efficiency and enhance user experience.

Why use blockchain-based smart contracts and not simply upload data to a central server managed by a corporation? Well, think of it this way. People are becoming more wary about sharing their personal information with an external party, and allowing it to manage everything for them, to keep their data safe, maintain professional business practices, and charge fair prices. And rightfully so. Such centralization creates single points of failure. We have seen countless cases of personal data breaches, misuse, unethical practices such as selling personal data to any third party that is willing to pay, outright fraud, data theft, and abuse of dominant market position.

A smart contract solution could involve multiple parties and service providers, each managing a certain stage of the process. One firm can be in charge of insurance, another one of cleaning, a third company can be responsible for toll collection, and so on. And of course, the company managing the car sharing service will be in the mix too, but it wouldn't dominate the landscape. A blockchain solution allows for decentralization of the value chain, distributing data and market power across multiple parties and preventing any single entity from becoming a central point of failure, bottleneck, or a rent-seeker that could abuse its market position.

Similar developments can be expected with ride sharing and hailing services.

In ride sharing, multiple people agree to ride with the same vehicle, which is usually arranged on short notice. This is another great solution, which helps people save money, preserve the environment, and socialize. Smart contracts are the obvious choice for such ride sharing schemes. A smart contract could automatically calculate all fees and value exchanges involved in the service based on distance, rate per mile, number of passengers, and any other relevant variables. It could allow for a quick and easy fare split among passengers according to the distance or travel time used by each one of them.

Vehicle safety is another area where blockchain could be beneficial. Cars are becoming increasingly autonomous, which means that their cyber security needs to be addressed too. Designing robust IT infrastructure for such internet of Things applications is becoming critically important. The decentralized and immutable nature of blockchain could provide great benefits for data verification. It could mitigate the risk of central points of system failure and outside interference, and thus boost user security.

Other areas where blockchain is expected to play a major role in the automotive sector are supply chain management, manufacturing, lease financing of vehicles, vehicle registration, monitoring and authentication, telematics, and many more.

Next, we'll examine how blockchain can revolutionize the tech space as we know it.

Blockchain and the global tech giants

Now, let's consider the future of internet giants in the blockchain era. Many of the hypotheses and assumptions we will make are related to a scenario in which blockchain turns out to be a game-changing technology.

The current internet space is dominated by four tech companies: Google, Facebook, Amazon, and Apple. This is a centralized model in which four firms control a large portion of users' data.

Blockchain, on the other hand, is a technology that propels decentralization.

Therefore, it is very interesting how users would react when new decentralized alternatives come onto the stage. It is also important to note that all leading tech companies are looking into blockchain now and figuring out how they can incorporate it into their business models.

This is a purely strategic analysis of how blockchain could potentially impact the business of the four tech giants.

Let's get right into it and start by analyzing Google and its business in the blockchain era.

Google

Google is the true internet giant; as of 31st December 2018, the company's revenue was $110 billion, and this resulted in $13 billion NET income. We should also bear in mind that revenue grew at a staggering 17%. The firm continues to expand:

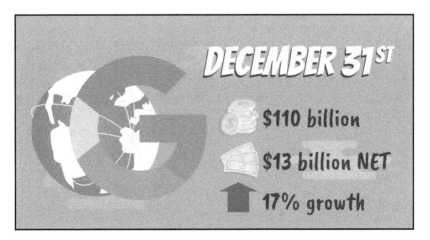

Most of us use some of Google's services on a daily basis, and it is hard not to do it. After all, it owns the most popular web search engine, video search engine, email service, location service, and the most popular operating system for mobile devices in the world.

Pretty much anything they do is not only world-class, but in most cases, best in-class.

There are two main reasons for Google's search dominance. The first one is habit, and the second one is superior data science and AI. Google established itself as the household name in search years ago, and people continue to use it when they need to find information. Moreover, the best way to come up with strong machine learning algorithms is to have a lot of user data in order to shape search results according to a person's preferences. Put simply, Google is able to find results that suit your search better because you've used their search engine in the past.

How could blockchain disrupt Google's search dominance?

It will be very hard to do it, and it will surely take some time. But that's not an impossible scenario. A growing number of platforms are trying to challenge Google's dominance. Privacy-focused search engines that do not sell user data such as DuckDuckGo have a good chance to disrupt the current status quo. But to do that, a search engine such as DuckDuckGo would need some sort of integration with a platform collecting customer data (the so-called identity tokens). Thus, by combining privacy-focused search with a similar quality search experience, users will be happier that one company does not own all of their search queries.

A further incentive is that a decentralized search platform of the future could offer users are tokens. Part of the advertising revenue coming in would serve as a reward for the platform's users. This could be a nice incentive that would help the platform find its first adopters and grow faster. We have seen similar models being implemented by blockchain start-ups such as the Brave browser with its native Basic Attention Token, discussed previously.

YouTube is the second largest search engine in the world, and of course the largest video search engine. Competing with YouTube is hard for many of the same reasons it is difficult to compete with Google search. They have tremendous amounts of data and can deliver users the video content they want to see.

However, it is also true that many content creators have been reportedly unhappy with royalties they receive from YouTube. In addition, as of now viewers are not rewarded in any way for the ads they are being shown.

How could blockchain disrupt YouTube's dominance?

In such a context, it probably makes sense to try to challenge YouTube's hegemony by introducing a model with stronger incentives for both content creators and viewers. Incentives in the form of cryptographic tokens along with attracting some high-quality content producers could help divert some traffic away from YouTube. Actually, DTube is a video sharing platform based on the Steem blockchain. It promises users several enticing incentives: a monetary incentive (earning tokens when contributing content), a decentralized platform resistant to censorship (users vote on video quality), and finally the platform is ad free. Not sure if this is the precise business model that will last and win against YouTube, but the first stone has been thrown.

Viuly is also developing a blockchain-based platform for video sharing and there are likely more decentralized competitors coming into the space:

Finally, we would like to discuss AdSense, Google's display advertising service that allows third-party sites to incorporate ads from advertisers Google finds for them. In this case, Google acts as an intermediary, driving website traffic to advertisers looking to post ads. Of course, Google collects a percentage of this ad revenue:

In general, people have a love-hate relationship with ads. Sometimes they find them useful, but in the majority of cases they are not. Moreover, the fact that so many websites make money exclusively from ad revenue has transformed the way content is displayed on the internet in not necessarily the best possible way. Many websites, even reputable ones, are full of clickbait trying to maximize the number of impressions users are displayed and boost ad revenues. This leads to a worse customer experience and promotes the wrong type of behavior, where website creators are not really interested in providing meaningful information, but in tricking visitors to make more clicks:

How could Blockchain disrupt AdSense?

Well, it is not impossible to see platforms such as Medium gaining even more traction in the future. An even better solution is a platform that combines one of the strongest features of Medium, user claps, with tokenized incentives. In fact, such a platform already exists, and it is Steemit.

Of course, it remains to be seen how ads could be incorporated in such a model, but a platform that's been optimized for user experience and helping people find relevant content without clickbait would be a significant improvement with respect to the current status quo.

We should also mention that Google is working on its own blockchain technology and solutions, just like all the other tech giants. We are looking forward to seeing how these efforts progress and if Google will manage to maintain its web dominance in the brave new decentralized world blockchain is promising.

Facebook

Of the four tech giants, Facebook's business is the one threatened by the advent of blockchain technology the most. People have grown wary of the amount of data Facebook collects.

One company controls information about the emails, biography, interests, acquaintances, relationships, travel, thoughts, and even love interests of a third of the global population. In April 2018, the Cambridge Analytica scandal confirmed and highlighted these worries:

The way Facebook collects data right now is the epitome of centralization.

Currently, Facebook is the second most popular platform used by digital advertisers. Its revenue was $40.6 billions in 2017 and the company managed to turn almost $16 billion into net income with an amazing 40% net income margin:

Its core businesses are the social media platforms Facebook and Instagram, and the messaging apps Facebook Messenger and WhatsApp.

Studies have shown that Facebook use does not improve people's happiness. On the contrary, it makes people feel worse. However, it should also be pointed out that Facebook, being a social network, benefits from really strong network effects. The platform creates value for its users because it connects them with many of their friends, relatives, and acquaintances.

How could blockchain disrupt Facebook's business?

A decentralized version of Facebook is likely to gain momentum. There are many people who simply wait for something different to come onto the stage. The cornerstone that future platforms should embrace is decentralization. If users unite around the idea that no single company should have that much control over their personal data, a decentralized platform's success becomes very likely. Right now, even if they don't admit it, Facebook manage user experience in order to boost advertising revenue. Of course, this isn't optimal for user happiness, and in fact, there are studies that have shown that people feel better when they spend less time on Facebook. A decentralized platform would have the obvious advantage that it can align incentives for users and enhance their experience, as well as store information in a decentralized way.

Facebook's network effects are really strong. More than two billion users already use the platform, which makes things much more difficult for new competitors. A decentralized alternative would need early adopters who would then spread the word and invite other users. In all likelihood, incentives through tokens could significantly help attract such early adopters.

Steemit is leading the way in creating such a platform. It is a blockchain-based social media where everyone gets paid for creating and curating content. In Steemit's model, users are rewarded for their participation with its native tokens. The correct market capabilization of its network is around $1 billion:

Instagram is one of Facebook's jewels, which it acquired for $1 billion in 2012. It is its fastest growing business line, even more so after the introduction of Instagram stories.

All comments related to Facebook are valid for Instagram with one major exception. Instagram is a platform that makes things pretty straightforward for users: they upload photos and that's it. The amount of data users provide on Instagram is not as much as that posted on Facebook. As with most blockchain-based alternative social networks and decentralized applications, a decentralized version of Instagram could incentivize users to participate on the platform by offering them tokens.

Many people remember Facebook's extravagant $19 billion acquisition of WhatsApp a few years ago. The reason Mark Zuckerberg decided to go through with it was that WhatsApp brings an enormous list of contacts who use the messaging app in a context that is quite different from that in Facebook. Nevertheless, WhatsApp collects a lot of personal information and quite importantly to Facebook, it creates a bridge between peoples' Facebook profiles and their telephone numbers, and even more alarmingly their contact lists:

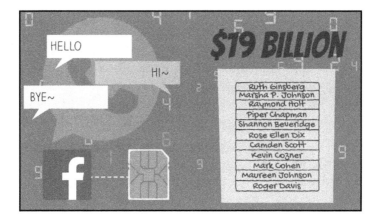

Messenger is Facebook's native messaging service, which is quite popular among Facebook users and is a powerhouse in the messaging space on its own.

Of course, it's not all grim for Facebook. Combining Facebook's platform with blockchain technology and cryptographic tokens could boost its customer value proposition. For example, this could greatly facilitate payments and marketplace functionalities on its platform. Or, it could help Facebook create tokenized crypto-economic incentives for its users to participate actively on the platform, similar to the way Steemit does. In fact, Facebook is already actively exploring blockchain opportunities and has assembled a dedicated R&D team for this purpose.

A great case study for them would be China's dominant WeChat messaging app with 800 million users, which is actively used for payments.

But one should also consider that at some point society could really get fed up with a huge social media company owning all their data and now trying to get into their wallets:

In all cases, in the next few years Facebook will either cement its position as the leading global social network or it will face competition from new and fast growing decentralized social media and messaging alternatives.

Amazon

Now, we'll focus our attention on Amazon. It is very impressive to see a company that big, which is able to continue to expand its business at such a fast pace.

Its core business divisions include the following:

- The world's number one web portal for e-commerce: `amazon.com`
- Amazon Web Services, an on-demand cloud computing platform, leader in its industry
- Alexa, a virtual assistant developed by Amazon
- Audible, an audiobooks marketplace
- Whole Foods Market, a US supermarket chain
- Amazon Prime, the streaming video and music division of Amazon

So, how could the advent of blockchain technology disrupt Amazon?

The biggest threat for Amazon would be a disruption to its e-commerce business. There are many blockchain projects building decentralized marketplaces, although most of them are not exactly for the consumer products you'll find on Amazon. These new challengers mostly focus on virtual goods such as computer game items, spare computer capacity, electricity, and so on. One notable new entrant in the e-commerce space and a direct competitor to Amazon.com is OpenBazaar. It was launched in 2016, backed by venture capital investors including Andreessen Horowitz and Union Square Ventures, and offers a fully decentralized peer-to-peer e-commerce marketplace where users can pay with multiple cryptocurrencies. It is less feature-rich than Amazon and other established market leaders, but it has zero platform fees and it doesn't control its users' personal data.

One of the reasons why Amazon is so successful is that it controls all the customer data on its platforms, which is analyzed and used to optimize consumer targeting, conversion rates, and revenue along the way.

As with most internet businesses, network effects are key in e-commerce too. Amazon has the critical mass and network traffic of many buyers and sellers. This is similar to a shopping mall in a prime central city area with a high density of people around. It has also the advantage of consumer habit and many user features on its side. This is a great market position to be in for Amazon, and hence it's among the highest valued companies in the world by equity investors.

However, the convenience for users comes with costs for them that could be substantial. These costs are both monetary and in terms of personal data. And as we know, data has become one of the most valuable commodities in the internet age. Amazon fully controls the platform and all information that passes through it. It can also restrict access to any third parties at will.

Decentralized e-commerce marketplaces could offer many advantages to users, including lower or no fees, control of their data, and unobstructed access to the platform. Let's see how far such platforms can go and whether they will be able to compete meaningfully with Amazon and the other centralized services we use today.

At this stage, it seems that vendors may have more incentives to migrate or diversify their distribution channels to such platforms in order to mitigate business risks and lower costs. On the other hand, consumer traffic may be trickier to attract, as many consumers tend to put convenience first and don't care that much about their privacy. At least for now… But this trend is likely to start changing with more public awareness and interest going into that direction, especially in the light of the recent scandals with Facebook, Experian, and other companies with widely reported data breaches.

Tokenized crypto-economic incentives in the form of bonuses or discounts and lower prices certainly can help attract consumers to new platforms. Moreover, tokens have the potential upside of value appreciation that goes along with the growth of the marketplace and network as a whole. In this way, a decentralized marketplace can share the value of its network effects with its users. This is the power of blockchain to align incentives across all participants in a network.

Whether decentralized e-commerce will take off and in what shape or form, only the future will tell. We can see the rapid growth of new entrants or a successful adaptation by incumbents such as Amazon, which may find good ways to incorporate blockchain technology in their business models. In any case, decentralization has its merits, from which users should benefit.

A good example how e-commerce giants are turning to blockchain comes from Alibaba. Alibaba's T-Mall platform is adopting blockchain technology in its cross-border supply chain to track and verify the origin of products and mitigate the risk of counterfeit goods being sold to consumers.

The impact of blockchain on Amazon Web services

It seems that Amazon is adapting well to the new technology and it has already created Hyperledger and Ethereum templates in its new Amazon Managed Blockchain platform, part of AWS. It was announced as a fully managed service that makes it easy to create and manage scalable blockchain networks.

A related project, Amazon **Quantum Ledger Database** (QLDB), which is a ledger database designed to provide transparent, immutable, and cryptographically verifiable log of transactions, was also introduced recently.

AWS and ConsenSys' blockchain startup Kaleido launched a full-stack platform dubbed **Kaleido Marketplace**, which helps enterprises implement blockchain solutions. The platform eliminates 80 percent of the custom code needed to build a given blockchain project by providing an array of full-stack tools and protocols that are plug-and-play, spanning needs from backend development to frontend app user interfaces.

In line with Amazon's other products and services, this should provide a fast and easy way to deploy blockchain technology in a corporate environment.

Decentralized web storage services could be a potential threat for this business, but again such new entrants have a long way to go:

AWS provides secure storage at a very competitive price and even US government agencies such as the CIA use it. So, it would be hard for projects such as Filecoin, Storj, Sia, MadeSafe, and the rest to gain traction with most of the established AWS user base, at least initially. Such decentralized storage solutions are more likely to be used first by other emerging decentralized applications in the blockchain economy. Nevertheless, the idea to distribute file storage across a network of consumer devices, utilize their spare capacity, and reward them for that with cryptographic tokens is very interesting and innovative. This is a continuation of the shared economy and spare capacity utilization trend we have been observing recently and can be a great opportunity for people looking to rent file storage space, and for those who have excess storage capacity. After all, AirBnB does a similar thing with real estate.

OK, great. Let's pause here and continue with the last of the four tech giants, Apple.

Apple

The release of the first iPod, in 2001, can be marked as the beginning of Apple's renaissance. The company went on to create some of the most impactful and beloved consumer electronics products the technology world has ever seen. The iPod, the iPhone, the iPad, the iMac, and iTunes sky rocketed the company's value and turned it into the biggest company in the world by market capitalization.

At first sight it appears as if Apple is a hardware company and it shouldn't be significantly threatened by the advent of blockchain.

After all, what does decentralization have to do with selling electronics hardware, right?

One of the fundamental beliefs of Apple's legendary co-founder Steve Jobs was that computer systems (and later mobile devices) should operate within a centralized ecosystem. According to him, consumers choose products that put together the best combination of hardware and software, and customers shouldn't be the ones deciding what type of software runs on their devices. This is what they pay consumer electronics producers to do for them. This insight that consumers value convenience the most makes a lot of sense and has been a key driving force behind Apple's success. Jobs also believed that iPhones, iPods, and iPads are predominantly software-driven and that is what made them so unique, apart from their beautiful design.

This philosophy though runs contrary to the ideas of decentralization currently gaining momentum with blockchain technology.

If people start feeling that decentralizing software applications and the economy overall is the preferred way forward, and Apple continues to exercise the same centralized authoritarian practices, this can be a potentially pivotal moment. Currently, Apple enjoys an incredibly loyal customer base among several generations of consumers. Apple's audience is so captive that it resembles the fan base of a sports club. Apple converts never change sides. But this following must be nurtured continuously with exciting new products and features in order to maintain its momentum across new generations of consumers. Shifting consumer tastes could weaken Apple's competitive edge. For the first time since the introduction of the first iPod many years ago, Apple cannot boast capturing consumer mindshare and leading the way with its exciting new technology. Instead, Bitcoin, Ethereum, and the rest of the blockchain crypto-economy have been doing this recently. In a scenario in which decentralization becomes as trendy as we expect, Apple will have to loosen some of its grip on its walled garden and allow its devices to operate with decentralized applications, or it would risk losing market share to a competitor that serves the needs of the market better.

So, that's a very interesting development to be monitored—how a decentralized economy would impact Apple's business model and how Apple would react or adapt to public decentralized applications, cryptocurrency payments, and any type of blockchain-related open source software.

On the positive side, Apple already uses blockchain technology, according to a patent it filed to create and store timestamps and protect secure elements such as SIM or micro SD cards storing confidential information on its devices. Essentially, blockchain could allow Apple to boost the security of its devices and applications even more. Right now, Apple's devices have best-in-class encryption. Remember how the CIA battled with the company over the encryption of an iPhone? Well, by adding blockchain technology into the mix, Apple could be able to raise the bar even higher.

Apple could also find opportunities in incorporating blockchain solutions in its ApplePay mobile payments and digital wallet service. Or, it can use such solutions to improve the content rights management and value distribution on its iTunes music platform.

Given the maturing and saturated smart phone market, blockchain may be exactly the right ingredient Apple can use to boost its growth once again.

Out of the big four tech companies we discussed, Apple bears the least business risks from blockchain disruption, given that around 80% of its revenue comes from hardware. And who knows, it may even manage to reinvent itself once again and come up with its next blockbuster product precisely in the blockchain space; imagine a hypothetical Apple iWallet, a new, high-quality, user-friendly blockchain wallet for securely storing crypto-assets competing with the likes of Ledger Nano and Trezor.

Summary

We have dragged this chapter on for a looong time, so I hope you haven't quit yet. We learned all about how blockchain will affect our day-to-day lives. We learned how blockchain will affect the financial sector. We learned about some of the issues faced in banks right now, and how blockchain will sort them out. We also understood how blockchain will disrupt common sectors such as food, transportation, technology, and many more!

I hope this chapter was exciting and illuminating for all of you readers out there. If this made you excited for the advent of blockchain, then our mission is accomplished!! Stay tuned, because the fun parts are just beginning! In the next chapter, we will look at how blockchain and AI go hand-in-hand and improve our quality of life.

14
Blockchain and AI

Blockchain and **artificial intelligence** (**AI**) are two of the hottest technology trends nowadays. No wonder most companies and venture-capital investors are interested in implementing these technologies in various areas.

Blockchain decentralizes and distributes data in an innovative and secure way with the use of cryptography. It can be used to optimize the efficiency of value transfer networks, asset registers, and marketplaces. That's why it's also called distributed ledger technology. A distributed ledger ensures that all parties in a network are on the same page at all times with regards to their past activities and current balances, as they update each new piece of information simultaneously. This is mostly a process innovation, which is very useful in the digital age when most transactions and business processes are managed electronically. Its applications, as we have seen throughout this book, range from financial services to supply-chain management and smart contracts.

We will cover the following topics as we progress on in this chapter:

- A brief history of AI
- Implementing AI
- Projects combining blockchain and AI
- Future of AI for smart contracts

A brief history of AI

AI, although a very common buzz word currently, is not a brand new concept. Research in the field started in the 1950s with computers learning simple games such as checkers. In the beginning, expectations were that within 20 years, machines will be capable of doing any work a human can do. Subsequently, progress in AI had its ups and downs, due to limitations in computing power and commercial viability, which impacted the available funding and public focus on the field. This should hardly be a surprise as it's a commonly repeating pattern in technological progress. A parallel can be drawn to space exploration with all the moon missions in the 1960s and 1970s, which have subsequently been discontinued or substantially slowed down. The public spotlight and funding budgets are a key driver behind continued innovation.

Coming back to AI, it was boosted further by increased computing power and commercial success in the 1990s and 2000s. It found use cases in logistics, data mining, medical diagnoses, and other areas. Another major breakthrough happened when the computer Deep Blue, developed by IBM, became the first AI to beat a world chess champion when it played with Garry Kasparov in 1997.

Implementing AI

Moving forward to the present day, we can see AI implementations pretty much everywhere around us, as more sectors are increasingly driven to automate tasks with smart algorithms. Some examples include Amazon's personalized user recommendations based on previous purchases or activity; Facebook and Google's targeted ads, Uber's AI model to determine arrival times, pick-up locations, and fare prices, and PayPal's machine learning algorithms to detect and combat fraud. According to the technology-research firm Tractica, which has identified over 150 specific AI use cases across 29 industries, the global market for AI software and services will reach $60,000,000,000 by 2025.

AI relies on large datasets to train and improve algorithms, and data seems to be the intersection between blockchain and AI. Data is a key resource that enables AI development. Blockchain, fundamentally, is a data structure that enables efficient ways of crowdsourcing resources through peer-to-peer marketplaces and incentive mechanisms that originate from game theory. Therefore, the first projects we saw that tried to combine both technologies revolved around AI marketplaces and crowdsourced computing resources. Given AI's enormous potential and the current state of the global tech industry, where market power is highly concentrated in a handful of very powerful companies, it may be a good thing to have a decentralized alternative for AI resources.

Now, let's have a closer look at some of the innovative projects that are combining blockchain and AI.

Projects combining blockchain and AI

SingularityNet, founded by the prominent AI scientist Ben Goertzel who also created the human-like robot Sophia, is building a decentralized marketplace for AI services. A good starting point for our analysis would be the project's whitepaper, which summarizes it as follows:

> *"The value and power of Artificial Intelligence is growing dramatically every year, and will soon dominate the internet – and the economy as a whole. However, AI tools today are fragmented by a closed development environment; most are developed by one company to perform one task, and there is no way to plug two tools together. SingularityNET aims to become the key protocol for networking AI and machine learning tools to form a coordinated Artificial General Intelligence."*

SingularityNET is an open source protocol and collection of smart contracts for a decentralized market of coordinated AI services. Within this framework, the benefits of AI become a global commons infrastructure for the benefit of all—anyone can access AI tech or become a stakeholder in its development. Anyone can add an AI or machine learning service to SingularityNET for use by the network, and receive network payment tokens in exchange. The architecture of a typical SingularityNet system is as follows:

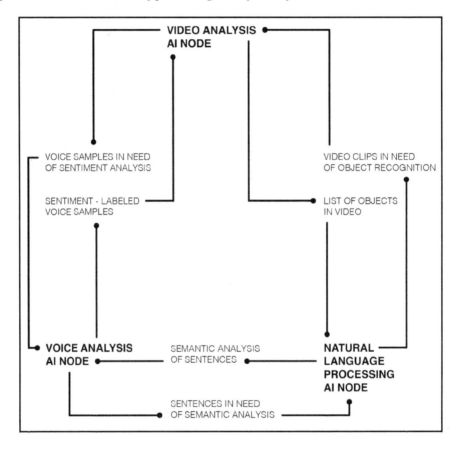

SingularityNET is backed by the SingularityNET Foundation, which operates on the belief that the benefits of AI shouldn't be dominated by any small set of powerful institutions, but shared by all. A key goal of SingularityNET is to ensure the technology is benevolent according to human standards, and the network is designed to incentivize and reward beneficial players.

The key idea here is that AI services should be made accessible and tradeable on a competitive P2P market for spare capacity just like AirBnB does with real estate. The unexploited resources here are AI algorithms and software developed by independent researchers that exist on GitHub and elsewhere, as well as computer processing power and memory. Currently, AI R&D is the domain of universities and large tech corporations, while SingularityNet aims to make it a shared resource available at free market prices to small and medium enterprises that can't afford their own teams of AI experts. Services exchanged on the platform could be software or hardware-based and may include the following:

- Image and video processing services, such finding out which people are in a video, or producing a text description of an image
- Language processing services, such as text summarization, machine translation, or text-sentiment analysis
- Providing datasets as background knowledge to train AIs to do data analysis of other datasets
- Requests to have a particular dataset analyzed
- Exchanging processing time or memory

As mentioned previously, machine learning tools require large datasets, which are difficult to obtain and manage. The closed development environment model of large tech corporations obstructs sharing such datasets. On the other hand, an open source environment such as SingularityNet can enable dataset-sharing in a secure, encrypted way. Therefore, it should stimulate the development of AI as a whole by boosting activity in the sector. An example of SingularityNET is shown in the following diagram:

Hanson humanoid robots, created by SingularityNET partner Hanson Robotics, will be early targets for embedded implementation of SingularityNET Agents.

There are also other similar projects trying to pioneer AI-related decentralized marketplaces or networks on the blockchain. One such project, called DeepBrain Chain, is building a decentralized global cloud-computing platform for training machine learning, deep learning, and other AI algorithms. AI-training tasks are heavily computationally-intensive processes. The machines running nodes on the DeepBrain Chain network can rent out their processing capacity to participants who need to deploy it in AI model training. Users can choose among different AI frameworks, such as TensorFlow, Caffe2, and h2o. The layour of DeepBrain Chain is shown in the following diagram:

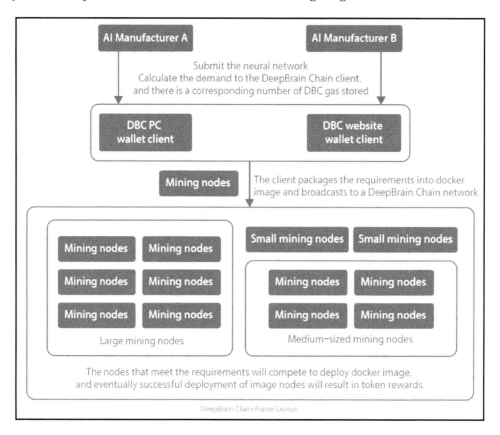

The architecture of the mining nodes seen in the preceding diagram is as follows:

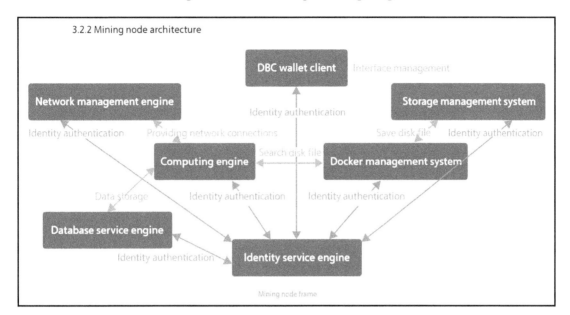

Datasets and AI models can also be shared and traded on the platform. AI models that have been successfully run on the platform's testnet include driverless cars, natural-language processing, and facial-recognition models.

Ocean Protocol is another project focused on creating a free decentralized market for data, mainly for AI development. Their view is that the availability of high-quality training data is essential to continued advancements in AI, even more so than new AI algorithms:

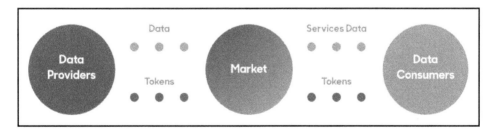

There seems to be higher availability of algorithms and a bottleneck in datasets for training them, so that's the problem Ocean Protocol is tackling. As a pilot project, Ocean is working with several automakers to collect data to develop AI for autonomous cars.

Here, we saw several examples of general-purpose projects that combine AI and blockchain. They basically use blockchain technology to create decentralized marketplaces for AI algorithms, datasets, and shared computational resources to train such algorithms. The added advantage of blockchain is data encryption, which helps protect privacy in a sharing economy. Homomorphic encryption can be used to protect both user data and AI models from being compromised in a cloud-computing environment. This refers to an encryption method that makes the result of an operation on plaintext equivalent to the result of an operation on ciphertext.

Future of AI for smart contracts

The more futuristic concept of AI for smart contracts, which eventually can be used to build and run AI DApps and **decentralized autonomous organizations** (**DAOs**) in such a way that they can adapt and evolve to complete tasks with very limited human intervention is also very interesting.

A project called Cortex claims to be the first blockchain to support on-chain AI. They've managed to deploy a couple of AI models on their testnet using techniques such as quantization and compression. Quantization is a concept in machine learning that combines lightweight inference with high performance, which allows AI models to be executed with high levels of accuracy and low memory costs:

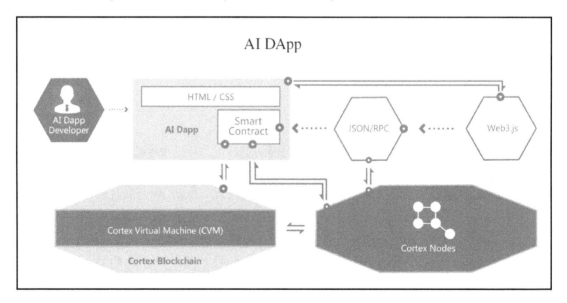

The inference process works as follows:

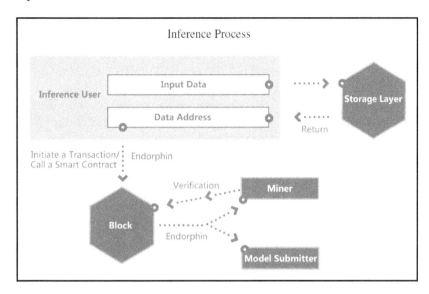

Compression reduces the size and data usage of models. The first model, a Cat or Dog classifier, was originally over 500 MB in size. An integer model was generated after transferring learning from the original model, to reduce its size first to about 130 MB and then to less than 15 MB.After training, the accuracy under floating numbers was over 94%, and the accuracy after full compression and converting to an integer model was over 90%.

The model submission process works as shown in the following diagram:

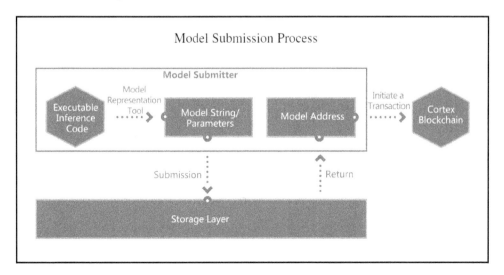

The second model does digit recognition based on the MNIST dataset, a large database of handwritten digits that's commonly used to train various image-processing systems. It infers data from a binarized image, giving a result of 0 to 9 with an accuracy of over 98%.

When tested, both models have been shown to successfully eliminate random factors in the inference process and give deterministic results to reach inferred consensus on-chain. These results show that some accurate and performant AI models can be deployed on-chain. Naturally, Cortex has higher hardware requirements for full nodes than Bitcoin and Ethereum in terms of storage capacity and processing power. The combined inference process on full nodes is shown in the following diagram:

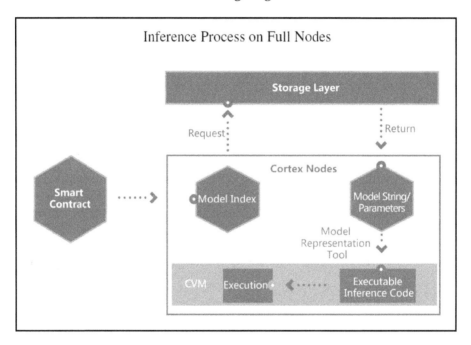

Future AI DApps being envisaged include information services for personalized recommendations (suggesting news of potential interest based on user profiles), image search engines, news/summary writing (generating new text based on another text), financial services such as credit scores (based on a user's online data) or intelligent investment advisory (based on financial datasets), AI assistants that provide automatic Q&A services (chatbots that generate answers based on human dialogue), and industry-knowledge graphs (expert systems that can be used in medical, consulting, and other industries).

Summary

Given the inherent data and computational redundancy in blockchains, deploying AI smart contracts at scale still presents many challenges and may always be inferior in performance to centralized engines. Still, some machine learning algorithms could be deployable on-chain in a cost and data-efficient manner to bring smart contracts to the next level. For the moment, the most feasible combination of blockchain and AI technologies seems to be for pooling computational resources together and distributing them across a network of algorithmic and data providers to harness these resources in a collaborative manner in order to emulate the performance and output of large, world-class AI companies.

15
Current Issues and Potential Solutions to Take Blockchain to the Next Level

If you have followed this book thoroughly so far, you should have a pretty good understanding of what blockchain technology is, how it works, and its applications and use cases. Perhaps you are excited about the disruptive potential of this new technology with all its incredible advantages. Ready for this brave new decentralized blockchain world? Well, not so fast, we are not quite there yet. There are some critical issues that need to be resolved first. In this chapter, we will be addressing those issues and finding potential solutions to them.

We will cover the following topics in this chapter:

- Issues faced by blockchain
- Solutions for scalability issues
- On-chain solutions
- Off-chain solutions
- Solutions to other challenges
- Next generation blockchain projects
- The exciting world of blockchain

Issues faced by blockchain

Decentralized systems are great in many aspects, but they are inherently disadvantaged versus centralized systems in the important aspects of scalability and governance. Running consensus among all nodes on the network just takes too much time and energy. Contrast this with a network with just one central server. Surely it will run faster? But we have already discussed the disadvantage of the central server model: it has a central point of failure. Therefore, there is a trade-off between scalability and speed on one hand, and security on the other hand.

Scalability

Blockchains, at present, are notoriously slow compared to centralized payment processing networks, such as Visa, Mastercard, and PayPal. Bitcoin's blockchain can currently process only up to seven transactions per second. Ethereum's blockchain is a bit faster and can currently process up to 30 transactions per second. Compare this to Visa and Mastercard, which can handle up to about 50,000 transactions per second. PayPal has registered a peak throughput of 450 transactions per second, as shown in the following diagram:

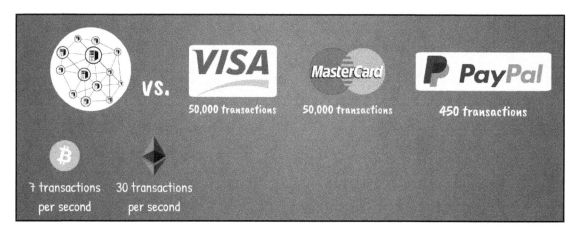

Clearly, one of the main scalability bottlenecks for both Bitcoin and Ethereum is the Proof-of-Work global consensus mechanism. Their current architectures would need some modifications in order to scale to mass-adopted general-purpose technologies. Of course, protocol improvement proposals are being submitted constantly by the global community of developers and the core development teams are busy working on upgrades. But the technical complexity is only one side of the issue. Another side is political, and here is where the governance issue comes into play.

With such broad communities of stakeholders, it is extremely hard to reach a consensus on the future development of a project. Moreover, the relationships between various participants are quite complex. Blockchain networks are not corporations where the separation of ownership, power, and control, among shareholders, management board, and other stakeholders, are clear. At least in this early stage, the governance lines in the blockchain community are pretty blurred. The list of important stakeholders includes founding teams, foundations, or other formal governing bodies, developers, miners, and cryptoasset holders. All these stakeholders jointly contribute to the value of the network. To that end, they form an ecosystem, in which each stakeholder group needs the other groups and they all benefit from their mutual involvement in the system.

In economics, this is called a **positive network effect**. The larger the network, the more valuable it is.

But the great diversity of the network poses issues when decisions need to be made and everybody needs to agree to a course of action. This has been demonstrated on many occasions, some of the most famous ones being the split of the Ethereum network after the DAO hack between Ethereum and Ethereum Classic in 2016, and the Bitcoin scaling debate in 2017. The latter unfolded over a large part of 2017, with the hot topic being Bitcoin protocol upgrade proposals regarding increasing the block size limit and implementation of a technology called segregated witness, both for the sake of scalability improvement. During that debate, a huge divide in the Bitcoin community ensued, which couldn't be resolved and resulted in a split of the network, known as a hard fork, between the original Bitcoin and the new Bitcoin Cash.

So, that's how we today have Bitcoin and Bitcoin Cash, as well as Ethereum and Ethereum Classic:

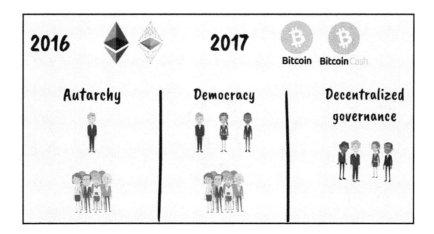

Governance

Decentralized governance is a quite complicated matter. Political systems have been trying to arrive at an optimal balance of power and representation for ages. And even after so much trial and error, this balance is tricky to maintain efficiently. Representatives are necessary to streamline decision making, but also create a center of power and render a much more centralized system than perhaps originally envisaged.

So, how can governance in the blockchain community be streamlined without compromising on its foundational principle of decentralization? This is the next big question after scalability that the new generation of blockchain technology is trying to resolve.

Interoperability

Another key issue for blockchains is interoperability. Currently, different blockchains don't talk to each other and even have serious difficulty fetching data from the internet. For that, they need special intermediaries called **Oracles**. Oracles provide an interface between smart contracts that live on the blockchain and any external data they need access to. Such data may be a critical condition for the correct execution of the smart contract. Therefore, centralized Oracles, being sort of middlemen, are not an ideal solution for a technology that tries to cut out middlemen and promote decentralization around the world. The next generation blockchains definitely need to be able to interconnect with each other, and with legacy IT infrastructure, in order to achieve global success:

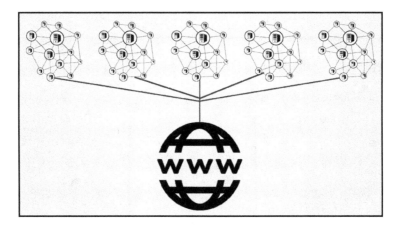

Privacy

Privacy on the blockchain is another critical issue that needs to be addressed. For example, the financial sector is so heavily regulated that customer privacy must be preserved at all cost and sensitive information can be shared only with regulators on a need-to-know basis. Similarly, many corporations interested in deploying blockchain technology in their internal processes probably wouldn't like their business secrets to be recorded on a transparent and immutable public ledger. The same goes for the private financial dealings of many high-profile or high-net-worth individuals. Privacy is highly valued in the internet age and blockchains must be able to provide this option to users if they are to achieve mass adoption.

Now that we have defined the main issues, let's look at their potential solutions. At the forefront of blockchain innovation, we have novel consensus algorithms such as Proof-of-Stake and its variations, as well as other cutting-edge technologies such as lightning networks, state channels, side-chains, sharding, plasma, multi-layer protocols, atomic swaps, and decentralized exchanges to name a few. We'll look into them in more detail in the following sections. They are being developed both as solutions for upgrading existing blockchain protocols such as Bitcoin and Ethereum, and as foundations of the architecture of newly emerging blockchain protocols such as Cardano, Tezos, EOS, Polkadot, Cosmos, Icon, Wanchain, RChain, Aion, Zilliqa, and many others:

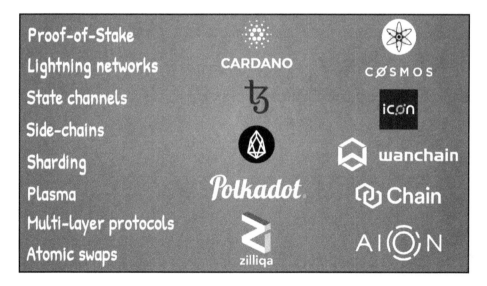

It's getting very, very interesting! We are going to have a sneak peek into Blockchain 3.0! Stay tuned!

Solutions for scalability issues

First and foremost, blockchains need to address the scalability issue.

What do we mean exactly by scaling in the context of blockchains? A core security feature, but also a capacity limitation, of public blockchains such as Bitcoin and Ethereum is that their protocols require every transaction to be processed by every single full node in the network. Every operation that takes place on the blockchain, such as a payment or a deployment of a smart contract, must be replicated by all full nodes. This is what makes public blockchains secure, autonomous, and decentralized at the same time. Participants don't have to rely on someone else to tell them what the current state of the blockchain is; they figure it out for themselves.

This puts a constraint on a blockchain's transaction throughput. It cannot be higher than the processing capacity of individual nodes, some of which may be quite limited. For example, some nodes may use less powerful computers, such as consumer devices. However, they are still very important to keep the network as decentralized as possible. We don't want all mining to be concentrated in large industrial-scale mining facilities, which would reduce decentralization and hence diminish the core value proposition of blockchain. This would make it resemble the current state of the internet, which is basically an oligopoly dominated by tech giants such as Google, Amazon, and Facebook, or the current shape of the financial sector, an oligopoly dominated by huge multinational banking groups.

Therefore, some modifications and upgrades are needed in order to scale blockchain technology to a global user base of billions of people, commensurate with that of the internet, and at the same time keep it as decentralized as possible.

Blockchain scaling solutions are commonly categorized into two types:

- On-chain or layer 1 solutions, which are so called because they involve modifying the main underlying blockchain infrastructure
- Off-chain or layer 2 solutions, which develop additional network infrastructure that connects to the main blockchain but operate separately from it

To give you a useful analogy, imagine that we have a speedway and we want to upgrade it to allow for faster commuting by vehicles between two cities. Perhaps this speedway passes through a picturesque natural landscape with mountains, lakes, and rivers. The road may be a bit narrow and its pavement may be a little rough and uneven, so it doesn't allow for very high speed. The road may also not follow a straight line between the two cities and have a lot of turns, uphill, and downhill sections in order to go around lakes or Climb Mountains. Now, there are two main approaches to upgrade this road to allow for faster travel and higher throughput of vehicles. We can either make it wider or improve the quality of its pavement, or we can build additional infrastructure, such as tunnels and bridges, to enable quick passage through mountains, lakes, and rivers. Or, we can do both, as all these solutions are complementary to each other.

This is the path Ethereum is following. There are a number of projects working on various scalability solutions for Ethereum, employing many talented developers. They go along the following lines:

- Layer 1 on-chain solutions include switching from Proof-of-Work to the Proof-of-Stake consensus algorithm and implementing a technique called sharding.
- Layer 2 off-chain solutions include state channels, a lightning network called Raiden, a new concept layer for scaling smart contracts called Plasma, and another solution for processing complex computations called Truebit.

The different projects are seen in the following diagram:

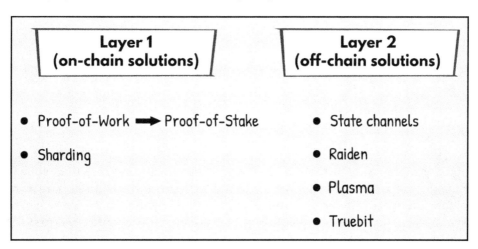

Next, we'll have a closer look at them. You can imagine that these new technologies can be quite complex, but we'll try to explain them without getting too technical.

On-chain solutions

As we saw in the preceding sections, on-chain transactions can be pretty cumbersome. For this, we will use the following solutions.

Proof-of-Stake

In this book, we have presented two consensus algorithms: Proof-of-Work, and Proof-of-Elapsed Time:

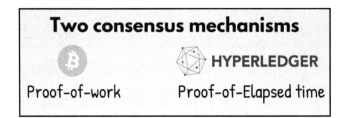

As we learned, consensus algorithms need to be suitable for the ecosystem they support. And there is a big difference between what is suitable for an open permission-less public blockchain, such as Bitcoin and Ethereum, and a private permissioned blockchain framework such as Hyperledger. The difference stems from the need for trust in the system, or lack thereof. Different levels of trust call for different consensus algorithms. Therefore Proof-of-Work is suitable for Bitcoin and Ethereum, but Proof-of-Elapsed Time is not. On the other hand, Proof-of-Elapsed Time is a great solution for the Hyperledger framework for permissioned blockchains.

An alternative to Proof-of-Work for public blockchains could be Proof-of-Stake. In fact, Ethereum's vision since inception has been to move to Proof-of-Stake, and this is expected to be implemented with the Casper upgrade.

Proof-of-Stake leverages a game theory principle of staking resources in order to mine new blocks, and this logic is similar to Proof-of-Work. The main difference is that while in Proof-of-Work miner's stake external resources, such as electricity and computer hardware, in Proof-of-Stake they pledge internal resources represented by their stake in the network's native cryptoasset. Thus, in the case of Ethereum, mining nodes would need to stake their Ether cryptocurrency in order to validate new transaction blocks. If they don't follow the rules of the protocol, miners would lose their security deposit of cryptoassets. This form of collateral should provide sufficiently strong incentives for miners to act with integrity.

The potential benefits of Proof-of-Stake versus Proof-of-Work are many. It doesn't consume enormous amounts of electricity, and therefore it is much more sustainable and environmentally friendly. It also should provide a higher transaction throughput as network consensus can be reached faster, perhaps almost immediately.

Proof-of-Stake and Proof-of-Work can also be combined in hybrid consensus algorithms. For example, the Proof-of-Work hash puzzle can be made easier for miners with larger stake in the native cryptoasset or who have been holding their stake for longer.

Actually, a hybrid consensus system is the way Ethereum pushes forward its roadmap towards transition to Proof-of-Stake. In stage 1 of the Ethereum Casper upgrade, all of the Proof-of-Work mechanics continue to exist, but additional Proof-of-Stake mechanics are added. In this implementation, 1 out of every 100 blocks is a checkpoint validated with Proof-of-Stake consensus. Participants who wish to be Proof-of-Stake validators can deposit their Ether cryptocurrency at a special smart contract address: a Casper contract. This address will provide them with a special validation code, which is a kind of a cryptographic key. The idea is similar to the keys used to sign and send transactions that we discussed in `Chapter 5`, *Five Forces of Bitcoin – #2 Cryptography*.

With this special code, validating nodes can sign and send messages, with which they vote and participate in the Proof-of-Stake consensus process. For a new transaction block to be approved for inclusion in the blockchain, at least two-thirds of the active validator pool has to commit to it. If a situation arises in which two incompatible blocks with conflicting sets of transactions are mined at the same time, the miners responsible for that lose their deposits, which represents a huge incentive to act in good faith. The cost of attacking the Proof-of-Stake consensus mechanism could potentially be even higher than buying a lot of expensive computer hardware for mining and engaging in repeated attacks on a Proof-of-Work consensus system. In Proof-of-Stake, validators also get mining rewards in the form of transaction fees. This effectively delivers a stable yield on the stake they have deposited. It is similar to the interest rate people get from a bond or a bank deposit. This **return on investment** (or **ROI**) is also similar to the way Proof-of-Work miners get block rewards when they mine new blocks, to compensate them for their investment in physical hardware and electricity. For a detailed description of this process, please check out `Chapter 6`, *Five Forces of Bitcoin – #3 Consensus Algorithm*.

As Vitalik Buterin, the founder of Ethereum, put it:

> "Proof-of-Stake can be thought of as a kind of virtual mining, whereas in Proof-of-Work, users can spend real-world dollars to buy real computers which expend electricity and produce blocks at a rate roughly proportional to the cost expended, in Proof-of-Stake, users spend real-world dollars to buy virtual coins inside the system, and then use an in-protocol mechanism to convert the virtual coins into virtual computers, which are simulated by the protocol to produce blocks at a rate roughly proportional to the cost expanded, replicating the exact same effect but without the electricity consumption."

Most new projects trying to build next generation blockchains use some variation of the Proof-of-Stake consensus mechanism.

The potential challenges for Proof-of-Stake come from the fact that it is a newer and largely untested protocol on a massive scale. After all, Proof-of-Work is a much more established and battle-tested consensus mechanism. This is evident from the 10-year history of Bitcoin. That's why the majority of alternative public blockchains, or alt-coins, use it at present. Whether it is sustainable to support a future global transaction network at the scale of the internet, based only on Proof-of-Work, is another question. Perhaps Proof-of-Stake will be more suitable for that. Or even more likely, we'll have many different consensus algorithms in use, each suitable for a different context:

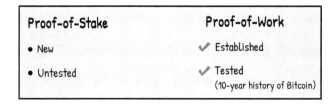

Sharding

Sharding is not a completely new technique in computer science and has been used for scaling existing distributed databases such as MySQL and MongoDB. The idea is to split all the tasks on the network into multiple chunks that are processed by different nodes. In this way, any single node will be involved in the validation of only a part of the blockchain, but not all of it.

This would result in improved throughput and reduced storage requirements. The basic process of sharding is shown in the following diagram:

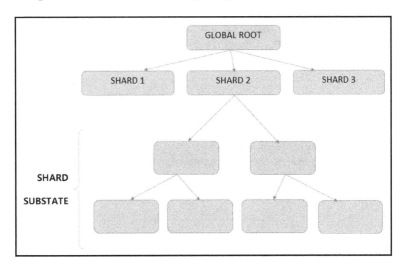

Implementing sharding in the blockchain world involves partitioning the state of the blockchain into multiple so-called shards. The state of the shared ledger can be split and tasks can be divided, for example, along account balances, smart contract code, transaction broadcasting, processing and storage, or in other ways. There are some challenges to be resolved before sharding can be fully implemented in blockchains. These include inter-shard communication and consensus on the history of each shard. Currently, sharding is an active area for research in the blockchain space, and some protocols are trying to implement it to varying degrees.

The plan for the next generation scalable Ethereum includes implementation of both Proof-of-Stake consensus algorithm and sharding. As Vitalik put it:

"The basic approach is to solve scalability challenges via an architecture in which nodes from a global validator set (in our case created through proof of stake bonding) are randomly assigned to specific shards, where each shard processes transactions in different parts of the state in parallel, thereby ensuring that work is distributed across nodes rather than being done by everyone."

Off-chain solutions

Layer 2 solutions are built on top of the main blockchain infrastructure. They do not require changes to the base level protocol; rather, they exist simply as smart contracts that interact with off-chain software. We will learn about some of these solutions in the following sections.

Payment or state channels

Payment or state channels are one of the more established blockchain scalability solutions. The idea is to use side channels or chains for processing transactions off the main chain. Once transactions on the side chain are processed and the state of the channel is finalized, it is written back on the main blockchain, as shown in the following diagram:

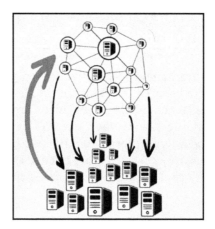

In this way, a lot of the transaction processing load is outsourced to a faster side chain, thus minimizing the amount of total validation effort by miners.

Here's a useful example to clarify this idea. Imagine that two friends go to a bar and open a tab. In this way, rather than paying for each round of drinks separately, their respective orders are recorded by the bartender and settled at the end of the night when the friends are about to leave.

Similarly, when two parties make transactions between each other in a payment channel, they will not record each transaction on the main blockchain. Instead, only after they finish all their dealings on the side chain will their respective account balances will be recorded on the main blockchain, as shown in the following diagram:

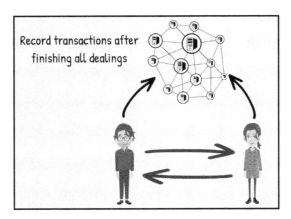

In a bit more technical terms, the process works along the following steps:

1. First, a part of the blockchain ledger, including the account balances of the parties involved in the payment channel, is locked in a smart contract. This smart contract includes the agreement and business logic of transactions between the participants in the channel:

2. Then, off-chain transaction processing between the parties takes place. The state of the participants' account balances is updated only between them for the time they use the channel. This allows any number of transactions to be processed without requiring the main blockchain, and it makes the process fast and scalable.

3. Once the parties have finished their dealings between them, the payment channel is closed, and the final state of their account balances is written back on the main blockchain:

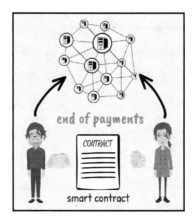

This is a very effective solution in rendering a faster and lighter blockchain network. Payment channels are a good solution for micropayments and IoT transactions, among other applications. They can minimize the cost base of transaction processing on the network.

Payment channels are used in Bitcoin's lightning network and Ethereum's Raiden network.

Lightning networks provide a useful platform for lightning fast transactions where participants don't need to open a bilateral payment channel with each person they want to transact with. Instead, the platform provides a network of such channels that reach everyone connected to it. Thus, a user just needs to open one channel to connect with the lightning network and then can transact with anyone else connected to it.

The Bitcoin lightning network has recently been deployed and is already operational.

There are also some decentralized applications that use state channels to great effect. Do you remember Fun Fair, the online gaming platform running on Ethereum? They have built state channels called Fate channels to enable fast and efficient transactions, and facilitate the scalability of their platform.

Plasma

Plasma is a new concept introduced by Vitalik Buterin and Joseph Poon in a research paper titled *Plasma: Scalable Autonomous Smart Contracts*, which was published in August 2017. It is similar, in a way, to state channels as it aims to build a platform for conducting transactions off the main blockchain, while it's still connected to it.

The novelty here is that Plasma allows for so-called child blockchains attached to the main Ethereum blockchain through a set of smart contracts. Each child chain, in turn, can have its own child sub-chains. This architecture enables many complex operations to be done by smart contracts only at the child chain level, with minimal interaction with the Ethereum mainnet. In this way, the scaling of entire decentralized applications can be managed. With Plasma, we can avoid the replication of every single smart contract operation across all full nodes on the Ethereum network. This solution would spread around the workload of transaction processing and make the Ethereum network much lighter and more efficient. The plasma architecture is shown in the following diagram:

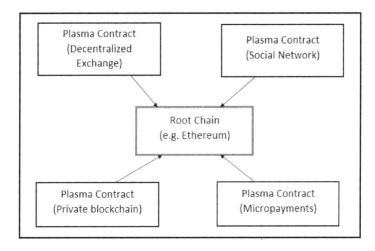

In Plasma, child blockchains can have their own consensus algorithm, which can be different from the one used by the Ethereum mainnet.

Plasma also provides a security mechanism, which guarantees that users can always withdraw their funds and assets from the child chain to the main Ethereum blockchain.

For securing Plasma chains further, another mechanism can be deployed, where validators or block producers on child chains commit deposits in a smart contract on the Ethereum mainnet, which binds them to play by the rules, at the peril of losing their deposit.

If we compare the state channel technology to the Plasma technology, state channels should still allow faster and cheaper transactions, while Plasma should allow more functionality and flexibility. Both technologies can actually be combined, with state channels built on top of Plasma chains.

Truebit

Truebit is a new technology, introduced in a research paper titled *A scalable verification solution for blockchains* published in November 2017 by Jason Teutsch and Christian Reitwießner. It is designed to facilitate very complex calculations on the Ethereum blockchain. This is different to increasing transaction throughput, which scaling solutions such as state channels and Plasma aim to resolve.

To understand the use case of Truebit, we need to keep in mind that computations performed on the main Ethereum blockchain are costly. Again, this is because they are processed by all full nodes on the network at the same time. To compensate miners for their computational work, Ethereum has a reward mechanism called gas cost, which is essentially transaction fees paid by the users who call transactions. Moreover, each Ethereum block has a maximum gas limit that sets a cap on how much total computation can be done by all transactions in a block. Therefore, some tasks that are too computationally intensive cannot be included in a block, even if they were the only transaction in that block.

For example, a smart contract running on Ethereum may need to verify that a transaction has been done on another blockchain, such as Bitcoin. This may be necessary for some applications that want to connect the two blockchains. Such verification could be a too big computational task to be performed on the Ethereum mainnet. In this case, Truebit can help. It essentially outsources the work on performing the verification to a third party. To guarantee that such third parties act in good faith, they are required to lock in a deposit in an Ethereum smart contract, which would be foregone if their job is not done properly. We can call this party a **Solver**. To enforce correct operation, the scheme makes use also of another third party, which checks the work performed by the first one, and has monetary incentives to do this properly. We can call this party a **Challenger**. In case there is a difference between the results obtained by the Solver and the Challenger, they are required to identify the exact operation that causes the disagreement. This should narrow down the computational work to a small task that can be performed on the Ethereum mainnet, and that would clearly show where the truth is, and which one is the correct result.

The following diagram shows the flow of the protocol:

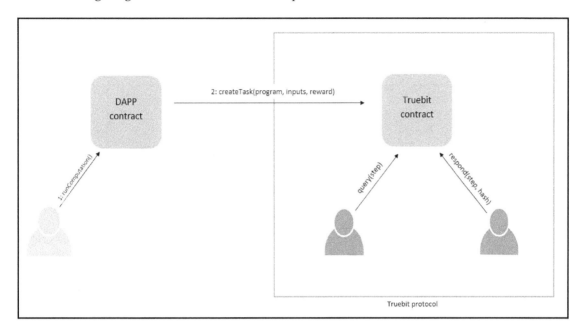

Truebit can be a useful solution to allow complex machine learning algorithms to run on the Ethereum blockchain, thus enabling artificially intelligent smart contracts that can be used to run decentralized autonomous organizations.

Finally, we should note that in all systems, there is an inherent trade-off between scalability and speed on one hand, and security on the other. For high-value transactions, perhaps it will always be better to process them directly on the main blockchain, for the sake of security. Small value transactions may be better served using the off-chain scaling solutions we discussed.

The next generation of blockchain technology will probably implement combinations of the solutions presented here in order to address the scalability issue.

Solutions to other challenges

Besides scalability, there are several other dimensions in which blockchain technology is evolving and upgrades are being developed.

Interoperability is a very important area, which is the focus of many research and development efforts. Various mechanisms for building bridges between different blockchain protocols are currently being tested. These include the so-called atomic swaps, decentralized exchanges, and inter-chain communication protocols, as shown in the following diagram:

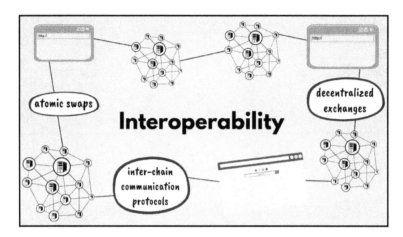

Atomic swaps represent a direct trade of cryptoassets belonging to one blockchain, such as Bitcoin, to cryptoassets belonging to another blockchain, such as Litecoin. This is done on-chain, as opposed to the majority of popular cryptoasset exchanges, which match and settle transactions off-chain, such as standard financial exchanges. This or other direct cross-chain transaction mechanisms are being deployed in the emerging decentralized exchanges, which are expected to become the main trading venues in the future.

Another important new development comes from Rootstock, which is building a smart contract platform for Bitcoin. The Rootstock platform is connected as a side chain to the main Bitcoin blockchain. It introduces smart contract tokens called **Smart Bitcoins**, which are pegged to the original Bitcoins. They are also compatible with Ethereum, as they use the same programming language, Solidity, and are compatible with the **Ethereum virtual machine** (**EVM**). So, this can provide a level of interoperability between the Bitcoin and Ethereum networks. Rootstock also implements a version of the lightning network, called Lumino Network, which can increase its transaction throughput to thousands of transactions per second.

As we discussed previously, privacy is also very important for businesses and individuals alike. One of the most powerful new privacy-enhancing technologies are the **zero-knowledge proofs** (or **zk-SNARKs**) pioneered by ZCash. Ethereum recently integrated this technology into its own protocol. This should create a privacy layer for Ethereum, which could greatly enhance its functionality. For example, it can enable decentralized voting applications on Ethereum, which inherently require privacy. Anonymous Ethereum tokens can have many other applications as well.

Actually, many of the new emerging blockchain protocols plan to include privacy features and consider zk-SNARKs as one of the best options for this. Such projects include Tezos, Polkadot, and Rootstock, among others.

Governance is another pressing issue that needs to be addressed in the blockchain space. Most solutions in that area revolve around Proof-of-Stake and various voting and staking mechanisms. Also, new blockchain architectures with different protocol layers, instead of just one protocol in charge of everything, are being designed to address the issue. In this way, transaction validation rules can be decoupled from network protocol rules, for example, and each dimension can evolve separately. Stakeholders can vote on upgrades of different parts of the blockchain protocol independently, which would promote more flexibility in its decentralized governance.

Next, we'll look into some emerging projects aiming to deliver third generation blockchains.

Next generation blockchain projects

Besides the upgrades in Bitcoin, Ethereum, and other established blockchains, there are many exciting new projects coming along and trying to build the blockchain of the future.

We briefly mentioned **Tezos**. It is described as a generic self-amending cryptographic ledger. This means that it deploys a decentralized consensus mechanism, not only for transaction validation and updating the state of its blockchain, but also on how its protocol and network are governed and evolve over time. To do this, it plans to deploy a delegated Proof-of-Stake consensus algorithm and to split its blockchain protocol into three distinct layers:

- A network protocol in charge of broadcasting transactions across its network
- A transaction protocol, which defines the criteria that make a transaction valid
- A consensus protocol that specifies how a consensus is reached around a unique chain of transactions

This should render the governance of the Tezos ecosystem efficient and allow it to evolve and update frequently to incorporate any features considered suitable by its community of stakeholders. In this way, Tezos can potentially include all the newest and best features developed in the blockchain space at any given time, and keep itself at the forefront of technological innovation. Such features may include new types of consensus algorithms, privacy features, on-chain or off-chain scalability, interoperability solutions, and so on.

Tezos is being designed also as a smart contract platform that allows for decentralized applications, such as Ethereum, but it uses a different programming language, and aims to bring some improvements upon existing platforms also in that area. Its mainnet was launched in September 2018.

Polkadot, led by Gavin Wood, who was one of the founders and **Chief Technology Officer** (or **CTO**) of Ethereum, focuses on resolving interoperability among blockchains. Polkadot aims to provide network infrastructure for interconnecting different blockchains. They want to build backbone infrastructure, called a relay-chain that connects other side chains, referred to as para-chains. Such side chains or para-chains can be other existing blockchain networks such as Bitcoin, Ethereum and Hyperledger, among others, as shown in the following diagram:

Since the primary objective of Polkadot is to provide cross-chain interoperability with other blockchains, it is not envisaged to support customized, complex smart contracts for decentralized applications in the way Ethereum does, for example. The aim is to keep the relay-chain as simple as possible, so its operation is optimized to provide efficient interconnectivity. Polkadot is expected to come online in 2019.

Cosmos, developed by Tendermint, is another notable long-awaited project focused on building cross-chain interconnectivity. It uses decentralized exchange technology and its mainnet was launched in 2018.

Aion is yet another new project trying to build an interconnected blockchain with bridges to external networks. They want to implement a novel, hybrid, delegated Poof-of-Stake or Proof-of-Work consensus mechanism, building on top of a lot of research and development done so far in the industry. They leverage concepts from Ethereum, Java, machine learning, and other fields of modern computer science in their aim to deliver the next generation blockchain technology.

Aion partners with two other prominent projects focused on building interconnected networks of blockchains, **ICON** and **Wanchain**, both from Asia. Wanchain also implements privacy features using ring signatures, the technology we presented with Monero. These projects draw parallels to the SWIFT system for international payments where each country has its own currency system, but multiple banks from any country can connect and interoperate through the SWIFT network.

Zilliqa, another exciting new project, aims to build a blockchain implementing sharding, the scalability solution Ethereum is exploring now. It also provides smart contract programming capabilities compatible with Ethereum's Solidity language.

Another new project that is trying to implement sharding is **RChain**. They are building a smart contracts and decentralized applications platform with a virtual machine and programming language, leveraging concepts from Ethereum and other recent innovations. RChain is also building a Proof-of-Stake consensus protocol similar to Ethereum's Casper.

Cardano and **EOS** are two other notable projects trying to resolve the limitations of existing blockchains all at once, tackling scalability, governance, interoperability and so on. They are both based on the delegated Proof-of-Stake consensus mechanism and enable smart contracts. They are currently at different stages of their development and carry high expectations by the blockchain community.

The pipeline of ambitious new projects is very long and covering them all is beyond our scope.

The exciting world of blockchain

We can now draw a conclusion here that blockchain is an exciting new technology, which is still in its infancy and naturally needs to resolve some issues and mature before it reaches mass global adoption. Blockchain has become one of the most hyped technologies in a very short space of time. There is a lot ongoing innovation in the blockchain space taking place at an accelerated rate. This new field has managed to excite a lot of smart people, which see enormous opportunities opening up. Talent and money are flowing in with strong momentum from all parts of the world.

Resemblance to previous disruptive innovations

The trend is similar to what we have seen in previous industrial revolutions such as steam power, railroads, automobiles, electricity, computers, and the internet. They all have gone through the cycle blockchain technology is experiencing now.

Besides the well-known issues of scalability, interoperability, governance, and privacy, the user interface also needs to be addressed. But hey, we all know what early prototypes of each of the other technologies looked like and how they performed. We also know how they have evolved afterwards to reach mass adoption.

For the closest comparison, just have a look at the early web interfaces and capabilities. At the dawn of the internet, it used to take 24 to 48 hours to transmit a text message because it was routed from one dial-up connection to another. And now we have instant global messaging.

When email first came along, it used to take 2 hours to cross the internet and reach the recipient. Now, we can livestream high-definition video around the world.

In 1992, there were only a couple of websites on the internet, and look how many things we can do online now: communication, education, shopping, entertainment, business, and the list goes on…

And on top of that, pretty much everyone has a smartphone now and can use these applications. Even many people who don't have access to a bank account can access all the capabilities of the modern internet.

The technology hype cycle

Blockchain is not a panacea. It is not a solution for every single problem in the world and certainly shouldn't be treated like a get-rich-quick scheme. Nothing is perfect, and that includes blockchain. Like any technology, it has its strengths and weaknesses. And also, just like any major innovation, it goes through a hype cycle. As we stand now, we can say that blockchain has probably been overvalued in the short term in 2017 and undervalued in the long term as of 2018.

If we look at the recent past, all new ground-breaking disruptive tech concepts from the internet age have followed the same cycle.

Internet search gave a huge boost to the web and Google emerged as the big innovator and winner in that area. Baidu then brought the concept over to the Chinese market.

Then, e-commerce revolutionized the global retail industry and Amazon led the way there. Alibaba followed and took the Asian market by storm with a similar concept.

Then, social networks emerged and redesigned the paradigm of social interaction and communication around the world. Facebook led the wave of new global competitors there, followed by Twitter, Instagram, LinkedIn, Snapchat, and many others targeting different sub-segments of the social network space. Tencent brought the business model to Asia and even improved upon it with its WeChat platform. These social networks proved an important point, that the social element is a very important piece of the puzzle for any media company and almost any other business venture nowadays. It empowers long-lasting customer relationships and boosts network effects, which create economic value and provide sustainable competitive advantages to any business. Blockchain builds upon this aspect even further.

Meanwhile, the **internet of Things** (**IoT**) gained momentum with the advent of smartphones and upgraded communication networks.

Cloud computing has been developing in parallel, also enabled by the faster and more robust internet connectivity. This changed the way IT services are delivered both in the corporate and the consumer space.

The next wave of technological innovation was led by big data, artificial intelligence, and machine learning—all very powerful technologies.

Huge amounts of human and financial capital was poured into all of these technologies, to an extent driven by the hype factor, but these investments also spurred a lot innovation and economic growth. The combination of all these technologies is bringing really powerful new solutions and improvements to the world.

The latest new frontier in technology and business is blockchain. Like its predecessors, it quickly became a buzzword, due to the familiar hype cycle and human psychology. However, it is a real ground-breaking technology, and this fact has already been recognized by most established businesses, technology, economic, political, and social leaders around the world. Like its predecessors, it is expected to deliver huge economic benefits, and perhaps its potential to change the world is even greater.

For public cryptoassets, the process of price discovery is currently ongoing, and the market swings in wild speculation up and down, unable to reach consensus on the present value of these new technological networks, as shown in the following diagram:

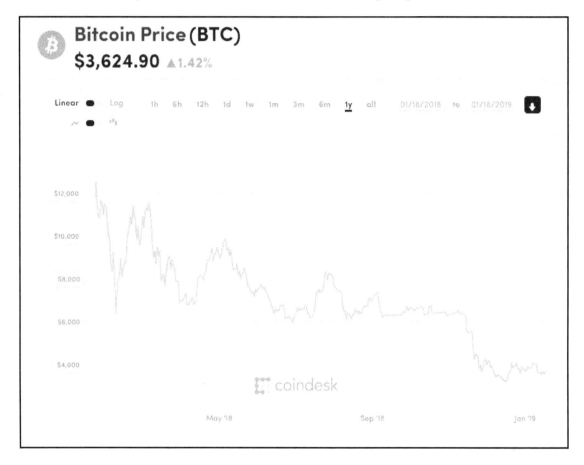

However, blockchain cryptoassets have the potential to gain global recognition as a new class of digital assets or commodities. They can have various functions such as medium of exchange, unit of account, and store of value, similar to standard currencies or gold. They can power the economy similarly to the way oil, electricity, and internet bandwidth do. They can also enable distribution and trade of various economic resources and risks like company shares. Since they exhibit features of various established asset classes, perhaps they don't belong to any pre-existing category but should be considered a separate asset class of their own.

Bitcoin futures contracts, a standard type of commodity trading contract, are already trading on major global exchanges such as the **Chicago Mercantile Exchange** (**CME**). Similar contracts are trading also on **Chicago Board Options Exchange** (**CBOE**) and are expected soon on NASDAQ. Bitcoin **Exchange Traded Funds** (**ETFs**), an established investment vehicle used for many assets and commodities, have also been in the pipeline for some time, and probably will be listed on the New York Stock Exchange at some point. These developments manifest the status Bitcoin is gaining globally as a form of digital gold. Perhaps other cryptoassets will follow suit, based on their further development and adoption. For example, Ether, the token giving access to distributed computational resources and storage on the Ethereum network, could be the next crypto-commodity traded in established financial venues around the world.

Blockchain technology brings a new paradigm, which is a huge improvement upon the current status quo in many industries.

The new era of decentralized economies powered by blockchain started with Bitcoin. It clearly showed to the world how value transfer can be managed in a decentralized self-sustaining way, unlike any other financial or economic system.

Then came Ethereum, which is widely considered the greatest milestone in blockchain technology since Bitcoin. It built upon the fundamentals of Bitcoin and brought about Blockchain 2.0 with many use cases beyond cryptocurrency. It enabled decentralized applications with huge potential economic impact. Ethereum's innovation paved the way to future sophisticated and autonomous decentralized economic and social systems. The new field of crypto-economics emerged combining economic game theory, cryptography, and blockchain with the power of the internet to create new types of connected global ecosystems.

Blockchain and Web 3.0

We are currently at a stage where a new third generation of blockchain technology is emerging. Again, it builds upon the previous generations, most clearly manifested by Bitcoin and Ethereum. The key building blocks of modern blockchains, such as consensus algorithms, cryptography, data structures, network protocols, governance mechanisms, virtual machines, programming languages, and so on, are being tried and tested, modified and experimented with in the pursuit of the optimal solution. And perhaps there isn't even a single optimal solution and the future global economy will have a myriad of different blockchains fitting different purposes. Most new blockchain designs evolve towards more complex architecture with multiple layers and modules that facilitate scalability, interconnectivity, governance, and privacy. The trajectory of this trend resembles the way the internet evolved towards a universe of interconnected public and private networks, and now we have the public internet and millions of private intranets. We also have multiple blockchain applications focused on solving different problems in various sectors of the global economy and society. The main difference with the current internet is that Web 3.0 should be more decentralized, fair, and censorship-resistant.

These new concepts hold promises to fundamentally change the way corporations and other organizations as we know them operate. The potential benefits for societies around the world are huge, from banking the billions of unbanked people to optimizing the performance of current industry leaders. All these improvements can not only create a lot of new economic value, but can also help distribute it in a better way, rewarding all participants in the ecosystem with their fair share.

As much as there is enthusiasm and optimism about the bright future, it is also important to understand that there is still a lot of hard work ahead in order to take blockchain technology to the next level.

Summary

We hope you have enjoyed this amazing journey through the world of blockchain. Our mission with creating this book was to try and increase awareness and understanding of blockchain technology, and its useful applications, benefits, and challenges. This new distributed computing technology represents an exciting innovation, holds a lot of potential, and shouldn't be dismissed easily due to the boom and bust cycle of publicly traded cryptoassets. It is also impossible to cover everything going on there right now. Blockchain is at a very early stage, and at the same time is evolving so quickly that new, interesting technological and business developments come up almost every day. We believe that blockchain technology is here to stay and expect to see some new major breakthroughs soon.

May Satoshi and Vitalik be with you! Thanks for sticking with us to the end!

Other Books You may Enjoy

If you enjoyed this book, you may be interested in these other books by Packt:

Blockchain By Example

Bellaj Badr, Richard Horrocks, Xun (Brian) Wu

ISBN: 9781788475686

- Grasp decentralized technology fundamentals to master blockchain principles
- Build blockchain projects on Bitcoin, Ethereum, and Hyperledger
- Create your currency and a payment application using Bitcoin
- Implement decentralized apps and supply chain systems using Hyperledger
- Write smart contracts, run your ICO, and build a Tontine decentralized app using Ethereum
- Implement distributed file management with blockchain
- Integrate blockchain into existing systems in your organization

Blockchain Quick Reference
Brenn Hill, Samanyu Chopra, Paul Valencourt

ISBN: 9781788995788

- Understand how blockchain architecture components work
- Acquaint yourself with cryptography and the mechanics behind blockchain
- Apply consensus protocol to determine the business sustainability
- Understand what ICOs and crypto-mining are and how they work
- Create cryptocurrency wallets and coins for transaction mechanisms
- Understand the use of Ethereum for smart contract and DApp development

Leave a review - let other readers know what you think

Please share your thoughts on this book with others by leaving a review on the site that you bought it from. If you purchased the book from Amazon, please leave us an honest review on this book's Amazon page. This is vital so that other potential readers can see and use your unbiased opinion to make purchasing decisions, we can understand what our customers think about our products, and our authors can see your feedback on the title that they have worked with Packt to create. It will only take a few minutes of your time, but is valuable to other potential customers, our authors, and Packt. Thank you!

Index

W

wallets
  about 80
  hardware wallets 81
  paper wallets 81
Wanchain 227
Web 3.0 100

wire transfers 74
wiring money 74

Z

ZCash 121
zero-knowledge proofs (zk-SNARKs) 225
Zilliqa 227
Zimbabwean dollar (ZWD) 17

www.ingramcontent.com/pod-product-compliance
Lightning Source LLC
LaVergne TN
LVHW081521050326
832903LV00025B/1569